Next Level Success

an essential primer for the real world

Interior layout design: Microarts
Cover design: Muhammad Umar
ISBN pbk: 0-9796926-6-0
ISBN-13 pbk: 978-0-9796926-6-6

For my mom, Joanie Shepard,
who has always inspired me
to carve my own path.

You're going to find yourself in a rut, and you're going to find yourself on top of the world, and the only thing that matters is how you react in that particular instant. Nobody emerges from a tough spot or remains in a prosperous post for long unless they respect that the work never stops.

What are you going to do *right now*?

So many times in life, people find themselves content with their position, and it's in those moments, those bouts of indolence, that one's current fortune, good or bad, very often takes a turn for the worse. If it was bad already, the downfall continues. And if he or she happens to be in a triumphant place, deterioration begins shortly thereafter.

That is precisely why I've written this book. I've been very lucky in my life, and I know that. My parents taught me right from wrong and the valuable lessons that would lead me to where I am, writing to you now. I've worked hard and fast, and my success has therefore doubled just as my failures have done the same. I have made the very same good and bad decisions that you have made.

You and I have a lot in common. We are failures. We are not tough. We struggle to embrace change. We are not great problem solvers.

Yes, you and I have a lot in common, indeed, and we have these innate qualities in common with billions of other people. Now, here we are in a place where we get to settle up and decide if we are committed to charge ahead to remedy our various flaws and imperfections.

A jaunt through *Next Level Success* can help you. Foreseeing a wrong turn or capitalizing on a right one is not easy. Choosing to make a change in your life is hard, to say nothing of actually having to implement that change. And treading against the tides your peer group requires a high level of courage.

More pointedly: I wonder how my life would have been different if I had a copy of this book years ago.

Wherever you are now—whether you are at the top or the bottom of life, whether you have succeeded or failed, whether you come from a family with lots of money or a family where your mom or dad was (or is) working multiple jobs to support the family, whether you have long, straight hair or pig tails—you and I are here for one reason: to take your life to the next level. That's it. That's it. That. Is. It. I am unconcerned with where you are now or even where you've come from, and you shouldn't be concerned either. Some people start at the bottom; some people start at the top. The question is this: "What are you going to do now?" You've succeeded, and you've failed. So now, here you are. What are you going to do?

There is only one person who can impact your life, and that person is you. The time to part ways with excuses is NOW. The time to stop pointing fingers is now. The time to take ownership of your life is right at this moment.

The longer you procrastinate—trust me on this—the longer you procrastinate, you will find that is becomes harder for you to move ahead in life.

Fifteen sessions. That's what you have here. Fifteen sessions to be taken at your own pace. If you take them to heart, study them, and put them into practice, your world *will* change. Your perspective will widen. Your demeanor will perk up. Between The Present You and Your Best You stands this book. Whatever it is that you want to do with your life is very possible, *if* you decide that you want to take the initiative to get there. Whether you are trying to make a sports team or get into the school of your choice or get a great new job or go out with that fantastic guy or girl you see every day, but just don't have the courage to approach, your potential to achieve these things will increase exponentially after having worked through this program. If you're in a hole, you'll soon find yourself looking down at it. And if you're currently a step ahead, you'll soon be leaving your peers in the dust.

We stand in *our own* way, and it's time to move aside.

This, the story of the Next Level, is a journey I'm proud to be taking with you.

Contents

One

Accountability

There is a reason I've chosen to lead this program off with accountability, and that reason is simple: we don't have it anymore. Accountability has been lost to the old school, the way it used to be. People *used* to be good for their word. People *used* to back up their talk with their walk. People *used* to say something and mean it. People *used* to take responsibility for their actions.

Not so much anymore.

Today, people are more interested in what's in it for them, and, as a result of this selfishness, they don't care about the repercussions of taking the easy way out. It's easy to say you're going to do something and not do it when you have other, supposedly more important, things to do. It's easy *not* to raise your hand and take the blame when you know a screw-up is your fault.

Have you been in a meeting for an afterschool club or sports team, where members were discussing different ways to solve a problem? How many times in those meetings, did someone stand up and say, in nerd-like fashion, "Well, quite frankly, I haven't been performing to the best of my ability. I think I've diagnosed the problem, and I'm working on it."

Ha. Get serious. We take the easy way out, and there are two things to note about this: first, this is lazy and selfish. Simple. If you don't take responsibility or do as you say you will, you are lazy and you are selfish.

Second, though, being unaccountable comes back to get us, *every time*. You can defer responsibility and point fingers as long as you'd like, but 98% of the time, the burden will come back to you. Louis Nizer said that, "When a man points a finger at someone else, he should remember that four of his fingers are pointing at himself."

Most importantly, when you are unaccountable, people grow to understand that you can't be relied upon. They look elsewhere for important tasks to be completed. When big-shots are looking for a team to build a start-up company, do you think they say, *"Gee, I'm going to go out and find a group of people to work with who aren't very accountable"*? I don't think so. Unaccountable people, inevitably, are ostracized from more successful groups and left to fend for themselves with the bottom feeders. You *don't* want to be a bottom feeder.

Think, for a moment, how this applies to your life. Are you accountable? Do people look to you to complete tasks? Do they have to ask you multiple times to complete one simple task? Or do you do it on your own by your own initiative? Are you Ms. Reliable or Ms. Irresponsible? When something is your fault, do you raise your hand, apologize, and make a promise to fix it? Or do you duck in the corner and hope no one notices you?

Consider your reputation. Are you happy with that reputation?

Generally, people fear accountability. We'd much prefer to take the easy way out than own up to our mistakes. It's not fun to take ownership of our errors against risking looking stupid in front of somebody or a group of somebodies.

And that's what separates the good ones from the great ones.

If you look at people who have achieved excellence in their craft, ALL of them are the kinds of people who immediately step forward to put the weight on their shoulders. "I didn't do that right," they say, "but I can fix it." Do you think that people like Bill Gates or Oprah got it right on EVERY first try as they were climbing their way to success? Of course not. They never have and they never will.

This applies in sports. In academics. At your job. In business. Everywhere. We. Want. People. And. Organizations. We. Can. Count. On.

And this applies to *you*. Your level of accountability starts *now*. Developing these habits now creates the person you will become and will either reward you or punish you as you get older. It's tough to turn off and on. You don't wake up one morning and erase a lifetime of unaccountability. It takes time and it takes practice. If repetition breeds habit, then your opportunity to accept accountability for your actions starts TO-DAY. Like, NOW. Like, RIGHT NOW. Like, 5 minutes ago.

Why is it important to be accountable? Well, for one, being accountable mounts your reputation. When you are accountable, you grow to be someone that people can rely upon. You want to be that person.

Also, accountability is contagious. Your accountability spreads to those around you. When you are accountable, people around you see that it is okay for them to be accountable as well. *Your* accountability holds others accountable. When you take responsibility, others see that they need to step up their game, that they need to be responsible as well.

In fact, I'll go so far as to say that accountability is the root of all of your future success. And that's why I'm initiating *Next Level Success* with this topic. If you represent accountability, not only are you saying to *others* that you can be counted on, you are saying to *yourself* that you can be counted on. And let me tell you, there is no substitute for that level of confidence. No one can take that from you. If you are accountable, you are saying to yourself that you will do what it takes to succeed, regardless of what happens.

Success. Starts. With. Accountability. When you are accountable, you are empowered, and when you are empowered, there are no restraints on what you have the potential to accomplish.

Accountability. Think about a story in your life. Have you ever let somebody down? Of course you have. If you break Ms. Cole's lamp, you have two options: hide it behind her filing cabinet and hope she doesn't notice. Or, you can march up to Ms. Cole, crumpled lamp in hand, and say, "Ms. Cole, I broke your lamp. I didn't mean to, and I'm sorry. But I'm going to take my next paycheck and I'm going to buy you a new lamp. An even better lamp. Your other lamp wasn't really that pretty anyway." Trust me, Ms. Cole will be much happier with you as a result. She'll know that you are someone who is human and makes mistakes, but she'll also know that you are someone she can count on. Trust me, you'll feel better. And trust me when I tell you that:

Success. Starts. With. Accountability.

Ponder, for a moment, how this applies to your life. Let's consider losing weight. Maybe you're overweight or maybe not. No matter who you are, though, you have to eat right and exercise or you will put extra pounds on your hips. And that weight can slowly creep up on you: if you add a measly two pounds a year starting at age 15, that's forty pounds by the time you're in your thirties. And that weight ain't easy to dust off when you get to your thirties.

Is it easy, though, to go to the gym and run on a treadmill for an hour? Or ride your bike for an hour? Or lift weights for an hour?

What about eating right? Is it fun to eat broccoli? Is it easy to prepare your own lunch when there's a McDonald's *right there*? Ahhhhh!

Nope. None of this is easy. But that's what taking responsibility for your life is all about.

Most importantly, after about two weeks of eating right and working out—taking accountability for your physical well-being—you will start to love your regimen. You'll look in the mirror and say, "Whew. I look good. Dang good!" You'll start looking forward to lifting weights or riding your bike around your neighborhood, and guess what else: you don't have to believe me if you don't want to, but You. Will. Start. To. Like. Broccoli. When I was 13, I hated broccoli. When I was 17, I hated broccoli. When I was 22, I hated broccoli, but a little less. A couple years ago, I started forcing myself to eat broccoli, and you know what? I *love* broccoli now. In an omelette, as soup, or just on the side of a couple pieces of chicken. Sometimes I'll put a couple of heads of broccoli in my pocket, and I'll forget about it, and when I discover it later, I'll say, "Oh, my! I forgot about the broccoli in my pocket!" And I will be happy for the rest of the day. Go figure. I love going to the gym, and I love broccoli. And the thing is, it all has started with me taking a little responsibility.

These decisions, the decisions to be accountable, become easier. When you are accountable once, twice, three times...every time after that will become easier. It will become instinctive. You won't have to think twice about it.

Accountability mounts over time. So, this can become more burdensome or easier to handle. It's your choice. Accountability, after all, is liberating over time. When you know that you can take ownership of your life, you don't have to spend time looking over your shoulder wondering who is watching or worrying about what you've done. Accountability, for you, can and will become instantaneous, and it starts with practice. You're not just going to go out tonight and all of a sudden be naturally accountable. But you can practice it. You can take responsibility. You can have integrity.

Ahhhhh. Integrity. That's the key word. *Integrity* is at the root of all accountability. How many friends do you have that you can trust? Think about it. Family doesn't count. How many friends do you have that you can trust? I'm talking about 100%, life on the line, you can trust whatever they say or do. I'm guessing not very many, right? Maybe one or two; probably not three. They say they do, but when it comes down to it, do you think they have accountability. Do they talk about people behind their back? Do they laugh at the little guy? Do they try to hide their grades from their parents or sneak out of the house? Do they play video games instead of doing the homework or chores they *know* they're supposed to be doing? Think about this? Do you know anyone like that? That's not accountability. That's not integrity.

Integrity is not just saying, "Okay, I will not cheat on my homework." Integrity parallels accountability, and that means saying, "If I cheat on this test, I'll probably get an 'A', but I won't retain the information. I won't learn this stuff. I need to learn this stuff." Do you understand what I'm saying? Accountability isn't always about the here and now. Accountability reaches to tonight, tomorrow, next Tuesday, next year, and beyond. *We* are accountable to what happens to us in our lives today and ten years from now. Listen, you aren't ten years old anymore. No one else is responsible for us and we are not responsible for the good or bad decisions of others. My mom always said, "You are the cause of where you are at." Truer words were never spoken.

The interesting aspect about accountability is that once you become accountable, you are taking actionable steps toward success without even knowing it. And you owe it to yourself to be accountable, to be a person of your word. It's fair to say that you don't owe anybody anything, but nothing irks me more than someone I can't count on. Do you know what I do with those people in my life? I discard them. In the business world, I am surrounded by so many good people—some who I work with and some who work for me—and I don't have patience for people I can't count on. If you tell me that you're going to send me a report by Friday at 5:00, and you don't do it...guess what? I'm going to find someone who will. It's that simple.

The paradox, I suppose, is that we often demand accountability from others, but not from ourselves. We spend a lot of time talking about how Susie and Billy can't be relied upon, but maybe it's time to look in the mirror. Susie and Billy will take care of themselves; maybe they'll make good decisions or maybe they'll make horrible decisions. Let them live with those decisions.

Focus. On. Yourself. First. 100% or 0%...no middle ground. You can't wake up and say, "Eh, I feel like today is about a 65% accountability day." No. Be 100% accountable for you. And then extend it into the group. Think "I" as part of the whole package of "us." Personal responsibility starts with *you*, and then it spreads to others. But it starts with *you*. Say it with me now: Personal. Responsibility. Starts. With. Me.

Think, "What can *I* do to make this work better for *us*?" Don't think HIM or HER or THEM. *Him* or *her* or *them* don't have any control over you, what you have the potential to do. They don't understand your level of personal accountability. When you ask "Why do I have to?" Or, "Isn't there another way to do this?" You are being lazy. You're not taking responsibility. You're deflecting energy *away* from you when you want to be attracting energy *toward* you.

You are asking the wrong questions.

Ask the right questions. *What can* I *do for him or her, for them or for you?* Ask yourself, *How can* I *solve a problem, or get to a solution? How can* I *foster a better relationship with my parents? How* I *can improve myself?*

It's important to understand a vital aspect of accountability. If you take *nothing* else away from this section of the book, take this away: generally speaking, people cannot be relied upon. That's it! *This is the world we live in*. When you ask someone to do something, you can bet that one of two things is probably going to happen: they're going to complete the task late, or they're not going to do it at all without being asked twice or three times or more. And that's if they even do complete the task. Listen to me: PEOPLE. ARE. NOT. ACCOUNTABLE. This is how it is now in your life now, and this is how it's going to be forever. Get used to it. Get used to being disappointed by people. And get used to being let down. People will break appointments; they won't pull their weight on a group project; they won't call you back when they said they would; they won't pick you up when they said they would; they won't send you that document that you asked for that you *really, really, really* need RIGHT NOW; and they won't show up for a date when you've spent the whole day getting excited about it. This is *going* to happen. It's happened to me; it's happened to my friends; it's happened to everyone I know. That is the *one* thing I want you to take away from this: people are unreliable.

Even if they are reliable, and if they do show up on time, you can bet that they are not going to exceed your expectations. This is just the world that we live in.

But this is not a depressing thought. Based on what we've talked about throughout the course of this first chapter, this is actually kind of exciting, because it means two things for you. One, you need to surround yourself with people who are accountable. Crossing paths with people who aren't accountable is fine; it just makes it easier for you to discard them in favor of friends and business colleagues who are accountable. We'll talk more about this in a later chapter, but these people—these accountable people—are out there, and finding them is incredibly important to the progress of your life.

The second reason that it's exciting that this world is full of unaccountable people is that *you* can be that person who is accountable. Being reliable, as I've mentioned, can easily set you apart as different from the rest of the crowd. The fact that so many people are unaccountable puts a premium on those who are accountable. *You* will get that job. *You* will get that promotion. *You* will get that major project that everyone else wants. *You* will get to hang out with special people, the more accountable, more successful people.

You can be the person who exceeds expectations.

Even looking into your social life, *you* will get to date the best guy or the best girl. Hey! Don't look at me like that! I'm serious. If people are trying to surround themselves with people they can rely on, I'm telling you that that amazing guy or girl who you have your eye on is going to come after you. You can bet on it.

All right, those are my thoughts on accountability. Now, let's go to the workbook. Yay! Workbook! *Sigh*

The way this is going to work from one chapter to the next is that after you have read each chapter, complete the ensuing workbook, and then take time to digest your thoughts for a day or two before moving along to the next chapter.

I've organized each workbook to take just ten to fifteen minutes. Don't skip this step. And don't skimp on your answers: one or two word answers aren't going to make you fully grasp the current concept. Hey, be accountable for your answers! The thoughts I'm sharing with you throughout this program are essentially meaningless if you are not taking action and applying them to your own life, and that's what these workbooks are all about. The chapters are about learning and digesting. The workbooks are about taking ACTION.

Today's workbook is going to focus on how you can bring accountability into your own life. What it is it that you are doing now that you can be doing better, to be more accountable? If you are already accountable, then how can you take your level of accountability to the next level? How, ultimately, can you develop more responsibility in your life?

Workbook 1: Accountability

Key points from this session:

- VERY few people are accountable. And this is where you can establish a distinct advantage.

- Being accountable is tough at first, but it becomes MUCH easier over time, and it is MUCH more beneficial to you over time.

- Every issue—from minor problems to major disasters—is judged by the actions that followed. If you accept responsibility, people will respect you. If you deflect responsibility onto others, your reputation will suffer.

- After all, bad decisions and mistakes are GOING to happen just as you are going to enjoy minor and major victories. The mark of the truly successful person is one who is accountable for their mistakes as well as their triumphs.

- It's not necessarily FUN to be accountable: eating broccoli or running 3 miles on a treadmill, for example, is hard. But! This is taking responsibility for your health.

- Accountability is contagious: when you are accountable, others will follow suit.

- Integrity is THE ROOT of accountability, and...

- Accountability is THE ROOT of your future success. After all, when you are accountable for what you have the potential to accomplish, you start to have the confidence that it can actually happen.

Leadoff question: In reviewing your notes from this session, what is the ONE big thing you learned? What is your ONE big takeaway? (This can be a story, a lesson, a tactic, a call to action, or, well...anything.) Spend a paragraph or so elaborating on what this meant SPECIFICALLY to you:

Acting on accountability: Over the next day or two, take responsibility for a problem or issue in your life. (And there WILL be a problem or an issue with which to contend.) It can be large or small, but look someone in the eye, and say, "Hey, that was my mistake," or, if you NEVER make mistakes, say, "Hey, I'm going to take care of that."

Discuss below what your activity was, and how that impacted you:

1. Accountability

Calling back to the chapter: When you are accountable, you are empowered, and when you are empowered, there are no restraints on what you have the potential to accomplish. What is one specific thing you think you can accomplish if you hold yourself more accountable?

Real world application: Think about someone you know in the public eye who is unaccountable. They might be a politician or an author or a movie star or an athlete. Describe who they are, how they are unaccountable, and how they are perceived by the public. Do they have a positive or a negative reputation? Is that reputation based on their accountability or is it exclusive of their accountability? How could their lives be more successful if they represented accountability? Finally, do you think their lives would be happier if they were more accountable? Why?

Real world application: Now, let's shift gears to someone you know who IS accountable. Maybe they are in the public eye or maybe not, but take the space below to discuss your feelings about their accountability. Do you hold them in higher regard? Do you try to emulate their actions? Do you want to be like them? How does their accountability directly relate to their success or happiness? Give a specific example.

Moving toward the future: It is important to COMMIT to practicing personal accountability. Anyone can do one or two tasks and feel good about what they've accomplished. Now, moving forward, it is important to make it a habit to be accountable for your actions—good and bad. Discuss (in a paragraph or so) how you intend to do this. How do you intend to commit to a life of accountability?

Two

Finding Purpose

What is your vision for your life? Where are you going? How does that align with where you came from? What do you want to accomplish out of your life? I'm not talking about specific goals, which we'll get into later. I'm talking in general: what is your motivation? Do you want money? Fame? Lots of friends? Lots of shiny things? Or do you want to sacrifice the fame and fortune in favor of making a legitimate difference in someone else's life? Or, are you *super* ambitious and you want to have it all: the camera flash bulbs igniting in your face and a boxful of thank you notes from some far-off land where you donated your time and energy to those in need?

These are the questions to ponder—at a foundational level—before we move on to more specific themes. After all, how can you set goals when you don't know what you're aiming for? What good is it that you have a fantastic attitude and a strong work ethic if you don't even know what you stand for? How can you build an outstanding team around you when you're not sure what you want your own vision to look like? Right? And how can you deal with various failures and handle successes, for example, when you don't know how to parlay them with your vision?

The hunt for purpose encompasses two core components: First, what am I good at? Second, what am I passionate about? At some point in your life, those two worlds will converge, and at that point, magic is going to happen.

Right now, I'm sure there are things that you are naturally good at: a sport, a musical instrument, acting, playing chess. Singing, maybe. Perhaps you're better at math or science than you are at English or committing various historical events to memory. Or maybe you're like my brother, and you're just good at everything. One of the projects we're going to work on with this chapter's workbook is listing the various activities where you're talented, and then listing the various activities where you're passionate and seeing if there's a way to find a point where they intersect.

First, though, let's try to understand why purpose is so important.

Purpose is important because we need direction. *We all need direction*. You can work hard, but what good will that do if you don't have a clear picture of what you're working for? You'll be running around like a chicken with your head cut off.

Strategizing your purpose gives you the opportunity to really see what it is you want, and that puts you in a better position to know what you're after. Then, when good things happen, you'll be able to capitalize on them. When bad things happen, you'll be able to deal with them much easier than if you don't have a clearly defined vision or purpose.

In fact, this applies to your life *right now*, well before you ever graduate into the ranks of whatever it is you want to do with your life. Do you sometimes feel like something is missing in your life, like everything in your life isn't coming together as it could? Even when life is good, you're thinking, "I could be doing a little more. I just don't know what it is." Well, purpose is the answer. With purpose, you are able to shift away from these negative-type questions to more positive ones. "Look at what I have attracted into my life!" you say. "Look at the difference I'm making!" "So many rainbows and butterflies!" Your energy level will rise, and your results will improve. Most importantly, one success will build on another; your higher level of energy will swing from good times to bad. You won't wonder what others are thinking or if your ideas are the most popular. Most important to you is that you have direction and that you are making a difference in the world. You're authentic, and that's all that matters.

Does that make sense?

Purpose, though, isn't necessarily just a motivation for a long-term goal. Purpose is about what you are trying to accomplish right here, right now in your life, by tomorrow morning, by next Tuesday, by next month, by next year. Purpose is both short term and long term. Purpose is a representation of your motivation. Purpose, at its root, is who you are.

So, for a moment, let's think short term. What is important to you? Grades, maybe. Sports, boyfriends or girlfriends. Your family. Going to college. Getting a better job. An entrepreneurial pursuit. Your favorite subjects. Music. Videos. Music videos. And this list rolls on.

Let's extend it a little bit. All of those things are important to your growth, socially, physically, and, ultimately, professionally. But what are you going to do to be remembered? What really matters to you regarding your overall view of accomplishment? Need an idea? Think about a difference you can make. An immediate difference. Consider someone less fortunate than you. It might be someone in your school, in your neighborhood, across town, or across the world. There's always a tragedy going on in the world. What can *you* do to make a difference in your life *and* someone else's life, whether it is a neighbor friend or someone living in a developing country across the world? What is it that you can do to make a difference RIGHT NOW.

Purpose is the means to the end, with the understanding that you might not reach the end you desire. Purpose is about the journey. And nothing is more important than the journey. The journey is *far* paramount to the end result. Purpose gives you both direction and guidance *and* the fuel to keep going on that journey. Purpose gives you validation when times are good and motivation when times are bad. Think about it: if you're just running around working to accomplish tasks, but you don't have any idea *why* you are accomplishing those tasks, then what's the point? You'll be on autopilot, cruising through your life without a clue what you have the potential to accomplish. I'm telling you right now that there is nothing worse than cruising through life on autopilot, passionless. That is a sad, miserable, lonely, despondent existence.

If, however, in good times or bad, you are able to revert back to your core purpose, then you have all the answers you need for *why* you are doing what you're doing.

All of the money in the world is worthless without a clear foundation. And that foundation is, you guessed it: purpose. Anybody can slave through years of school or work a seventy hour week in order to live in a nice house and drive a nice car. But does what you're doing matter? Are you making a difference? Think about that as you move forward throughout today's chapter and beyond: if you want pretty things, you can have them, but is what you're doing having an impact? It's great to have a boat and go on cool vacations, but when you come back home, are you on a worthwhile pursuit to be an influence on the world around you?

Think Happiness. Now. It's *not* realistic for you to say things like:

"Once I get an A in this class, I'll be happy."

"Once I go to college, I'll be happy."

"Once I have a nice job, I'll be happy."

"Once I have a pretty wife, I'll be happy."

"Once I have a fat, steady paycheck, I'll be happy."

It doesn't work like that. You need to have happiness *now* before you can enjoy happiness *later*. Develop your happiness first. Happiness is being at peace with yourself, and a clearly defined purpose is your ticket to that peace. No matter what life throws at you, your purpose levies the understanding that you're on the right path. THAT is happiness: knowing that what you're doing matters. Happiness can be multiplied by success or money or a lucky break here or there, but without a solid foundation—without a solid purpose—happiness is hard to come by.

One word that you'll notice me using throughout the course of this chapter is DISCOVER. You *discover* your purpose from within. It doesn't magically appear. You don't pick up a shell one day on the beach and say, "Oh, hey! There's my purpose! I knew I'd find it somewhere!" Your purpose will come to you after you have done the due diligence to consider it, ponder it, evaluate it, and nurture it. And then do all these things over again.

This is starting to sound like a pet that you look after, that you have to feed in the morning and walk in the afternoon. Well, maybe it is. Your purpose needs care. Your purpose needs your attention just like your dog would. You might have to change the litter box for your purpose just like you would your cat. Your purpose is growing and changing, and you need to grow and change with it, but the only way you can do that is by taking the time to give it the consideration it deserves.

And indeed, once you've started to represent your purpose, you will start to attract others who have a similar purpose. Representing your purpose will be infectious. You'll be able to build or join a team who shares a similar direction. That can be a pretty powerful force.

Check it out: when you are sitting down to work on your purpose, consider your passion *first* and your talent *second*. Your passion is much, much, much more important than your talent. After all, if you busy yourself doing something that you happen to be good at—but you don't love—you are going to be miserable. *Crazy* miserable. Happiness stems from your passion, and then, hopefully, at some point, your talent will converge with it. Or at least you will work to develop the skills necessary to align with your passion.

Listen, as long as *you* are waking up in the morning with direction, with purpose, with passion, it doesn't matter if you're good at something or not. You'll become good. Trust me. If you love something enough, it will be *easy* for you to put in the hours to work to learn a trade or skill or craft. You will improve. But it starts with passion *first*.

Okay, so let's extend this even further and talk about how helping yourself and helping others work directly, hand in hand, every time.

The energy you put out via your purpose is going to come back to you, and this is going to be very, very, very important to your success. Because, even when you enjoy a string of success—a long and nothing-bad-is-ever-going-to-happen string of success—you are going to hit a roadblock. It's inevitable. And this is when your purpose will either come into focus or blow up in your face. If your intention is sound, sincere, and compassionate, you will ride out the tough times. If your intention is greedy, selfish, and inconsiderate, you're going to struggle.

I'll give you an example: when I got out of college, I left home to live a social experiment and write my first book, *Scratch Beginnings*. I self-published it and enjoyed a pretty fair amount of success: I went on the Today Show, CNN, Fox News, NPR, 20/20, and yada, yada, yada. I was getting invited to speak at corporate dinners and colleges and high school retreats. The book was used as a common read at many schools, and it was translated into Chinese. I was on top of the world. Girls loved me. Guys loved me. Everybody loved me.

Fast forward two years, and the well dried up. No more media. No more speaking. No more money. No more hot dates. I wasn't depressed, but I was unbelievably frustrated. All of the good times were gone. Then, I got an email from one of my old teachers. It's titled "Inspiring":

> I don't know if you even remember me, Adam, but I was a teacher at Southeast. A couple of weeks ago, I was at a teaching conference in RTP. A student was asked to speak about his success and motivation to the hundreds of teachers in attendance. He mentioned meeting and talking to you as one of his life-changing moments. How wonderful is it that you have that kind of impact on others!
> Regards, Ms. Kellogg

Now, how crazy is that? There I was, discouraged, searching for direction, not understanding what was next for me, or even what my own purpose was. I knew I could make a lot of money in the corporate world, but that wouldn't make me happy; it wouldn't give me direction; it wouldn't allow me to *truly* help others. So, there I was, having lost traction, not understanding if my purpose—my life's mission—was playing out for me. And that one email refocused me. That simple, one paragraph email from a teacher I hadn't heard from in years. One kid out there mentioned how meeting *me*—little old me!—was one of his life-changing moments. I printed that email, and I wrote at the bottom, "Remember WHY you do what you do." I hung it on my wall, and it stays there. It will stay there forever. It gives me perspective that what I do is not about me. My life's purpose is not about me. My life's purpose is about serving others.

Now, I didn't tell you about this email from Ms. Kellogg to impress you. Actually, the opposite. You have to understand that everyone, top to bottom, the greatest successes to the greatest failures, loses focus of their purpose. And the point is that they each, individually—you (!) each, individually—have the option to take a look at your direction, your intention, and to reconnect. In tough times, take a moment to yourself. Lock yourself in a dark room and breathe deep for ten minutes. Take a walk with no music and no phone. Lay out in the sun with nothing but the sound of the clouds. GET. IN. TOUCH. WITH. YOUR. PURPOSE. It's there, and it is what will allow you to refuel. Because listen, someone out there is waiting to be inspired by you. Someone will one day say that their life-changing moment was meeting you, and you want to be ready for that moment.

Got it? Cool.

Okay, so what are my three takeaways from this chapter: One, purpose gives meaning. With a clear motive and direction, you will have a much better understanding of what you're after.

Two, purpose breeds happiness. If you have purpose, then you are giving yourself a chance to be happy. And if you're giving yourself a chance to be happy, you're giving yourself a *much* better chance at being successful.

And third, it can be very easy to lose sight of your purpose. Don't let it slip away, slowly, day by day. Grasp it. Hold on to it. If you disconnect from your purpose for a moment, for an hour, for one exchange, that's fine. You can quickly reconnect. But if you fail to reconnect, if you string together a series of moments where you lose sight of your purpose, it will be easy to let it go. And this can be detrimental to your inevitable success.

One more note before we move along to the workbook. Discovering your purpose is the easy part. Anybody can sit down and say with their pompous, nerdy voice, "Uh, well, I live life with love and energy and I want to have a positive impact and I want to always be working on one major project." Fair enough. But! Once you've unearthed your purpose, the most important aspect is to hold fast to it. Represent it every day. Empty words on paper can actually have a negative effect as you start to allow your purpose to slip. REPRESENT. YOUR. PURPOSE. EVERY. DAY. When times are good, represent your purpose. And it won't matter so much when times are bad, because you know that you have a clear direction, that you know where you're headed, you know what you represent. Having purpose will catapult you in good times and allow you to work through the tough ones.

Your purpose is not permanent and it isn't your destiny. Your purpose is evolving...maybe on a yearly basis, maybe longer. It's important to understand that you need to revisit your purpose over time rather than accepting it as your lifelong destiny. You may discover that you are called to a greater purpose, you may learn that you're after a completely different purpose altogether, or you may find, as time passes, that the same purposes maintains forever.

The point is that some people don't manage their purpose well, and therefore, let it slip. They lose focus. Just as it's *not* easy to find purpose it *is* easy to lose it. How contradictory is that? It's tough to find and easy to lose. What a pain, right?

But this won't be you. You're different. You're not going to lose your purpose. You're going to *own* your purpose. Wake up every day and recite it. Write it on a piece of paper and tape it to your bathroom mirror. Tattoo it on your forehead. Okay, maybe not that, but you get the idea that you need to OWN. YOUR. PURPOSE. And when you start to lose sight of it a little, you're going to take ten minutes to sit alone in a dark room and reconnect with it. It *really* is that simple.

After all, this—your purpose—is who you are.

Workbook 2: Finding Purpose

Key points from this session:

- Establishing your purpose—at a foundational level—is key before moving along to more specific things (such as goal setting, for example).
- Purpose allows us to have a general focus on where we'd like to be heading.
- Finding your purpose encompasses two core components:
    1. What am I good at?
    2. What am I passionate about?
- Ideally, at some point, those two worlds will converge.
- Finding your purpose is a matter of getting in touch with what you REALLY want to do, regardless of fame, fortune, or anything else superficial.
- Determining the direction you're heading LONG-term allows you to focus on what you can be working on in the SHORT-term.
- Purpose is about the journey, rather than the end result. Maybe you have fame and fortune or maybe not, but at least you will be doing meaningful work.
- Your purpose allows you to help YOURSELF and help OTHERS.
- When you are discouraged, your purpose can help you pull through and refocus.
- Purpose breeds happiness.

Leadoff question: This was a heavy session on purpose. A lot of ideas were presented, and there are a lot of tactics to practice.

And it's true that defining your purpose takes time, but what is the ONE major thing you were able to take away from session number two? (This can be a story, a lesson, a tactic, a call to action, or...anything.) Spend a paragraph or so elaborating on what this session meant SPECIFICALLY to you:

The world around you: Think of one successful person you know, someone you admire. It could be someone famous, in the limelight, or someone behind the scenes like an engineer or a banker.

Think back to a time when he or she was younger, before he or she was successful. What do you think their purpose was? You can see where they are now, what they've accomplished, but consider where their mindset was long before they had enjoyed the success that they now have enjoyed. They were YOU, once upon a time, right?

2. Finding Purpose

Discovering your purpose:

List the 5 things that you are MOST PASSIONATE about:

Now, list the 5 things that you are MOST SKILLED at:

As you are working through the next activity, consider where the two lists above may converge. Surely, they do at some point, even if you don't have the *exact* same thing on each list.

Starting to define your purpose: As discussed in the chapter, your purpose may not come to you directly as you sit down to brainstorm ideas. Your purpose is evolving, and it may take a little while for it to come to you. That said, let's start the process here.

Start with the end in mind. Plan backwards. Where do you want to be in twenty years, ten years, five years, one year, next week? How can your purpose NOW reflect your journey to get to where you want to be? As said during the chapter, your purpose is ever-evolving, and it's true that it SHOULD develop over time. But! You can still plan for the future and change things up along the way...

Who do you want to help?

How can you help them?

What do you have to do NOW to get to the point where you can help them?

How can you help yourself in the process?

How can you enjoy yourself in the process?

What can you do—personally—to make these things happen?

If you don't make it to your end destination (if you're only able to help *fifty* people instead of *fifty thousand*, for example), will you be satisfied that you made a difference? Will you be proud of the journey? Will your purpose be enough to carry you along? Elaborate on why or why not?

Real world application: Write down your purpose and tape it on the wall NEXT TO your bed where you can see it every day. Each night before you go to sleep, recite it. When you wake up, while you're getting dressed, recite it.

And as it evolves, write down your new purpose and tape it next to your bed.

Once you have a core purpose on paper, sit in a dark room by yourself for five minutes. No TV, no music, no light. Close your eyes, and consider your purpose and how you plan to commit to enacting it every day. OWN YOUR PURPOSE!

Three

Dealing with Rejection and Failure

We're rolling here. Life is good. We've completed the first two sections and now we are in the zone. You're accountable. You have a better idea of what your purpose is going to be, even if you obviously haven't 100% nailed it down yet. You're a better person already, *and* you have set yourself up for success—and that took—what?—a week?

Solid.

Today we're diving into section number 3: *Dealing with Rejection and Failure*. Now this, ladies and gentlemen, here and now, is my specialty. This is my bread and butter. I know what I'm talking about when it comes to failure and rejection. When I was in the 8th grade, my science teacher said to me, just before the end of the school year: "Adam, your promotion to high school will be a happy day for me."

Listen, I have lived through more failure than most people you know, and I've been rejected by more sources—by business colleagues, by universities, by coaches, by literary agents, and by girls—than I care to remember. Let's just say I've spent most of my professional life in receipt of all of a variety of rebuffs and denials, dismissals and defeat. And I've learned from every experience, so that the next rejection or failure wasn't as painful. Or at least I was better-prepared to handle it.

What I want you to understand, more than anything, after working through this chapter, is that it doesn't matter where you come from. It doesn't matter if you come from a wealthy, silver spoon background, the poor side of the tracks, or anywhere in between. Everybody, on every level, deals with failure, and everybody, on every level deals with rejection. It's inevitable. It's going to happen, I can assure you. Guaranteed. Guaranteed. 100%, no questions asked, you are a failure. You've experienced failure before, but let me tell you, you're going to experience it again. And again. And again. It's coming. Maybe you're not at the top of the class, or maybe you're a budding valedictorian and a star field hockey player. Doesn't matter. As we'll talk about, the best of the best fail, and the only thing you can hope for is to be prepared for it when it comes, rather than saying, "Ugh. Failure? This sucks. I'm not supposed to fail!"

I want you to think about something: Without the risk of failure, there is no opportunity for success. Bam! Think about *that* for a second. Without the risk of failure, there is no opportunity for success. That is an intense statement, even as simple as it is. But think about it. Think about one place where you could potentially enjoy success without putting *something* on the line. You can't do it. If you are accepting the responsibility of working hard, of being vulnerable, of exerting energy toward a goal, you are taking a risk of both failure and success. There is a chance that you are going to fail, and there is a chance that you are going to succeed.

Now, certainly, your odds of succeeding and failing are variable, depending on the situation and different circumstances. Either way, though, no matter what the scale of success or failure is, you are still putting yourself out there, at the risk of failure. Without. The. Risk. Of. Failure. There. Is. No. Opportunity. For. Success. It's important to understand this. This will clear your mind from a lot of thoughts about impending failure. Think about it: if you're going into a situation, and you're thinking, "Something could go wrong with this. This might not end well. What if something goes wrong?", you're in trouble. If you're focused on the negative—the rejection or the failure—you'll get inside your head, and you'll talk your way out of success.

Because listen, something *is* going to go wrong. Something *is* going to go bad. It's inevitable! But if you know this—if you go into it thinking you're going to have some tough times to deal with—you have a much better handle on how you can deal with it and move on.

If you understand that you are going to make mistakes, then you understand that you don't have to be deterred by the journey *or* the end result. Good things are going to happen. Bad things are going to happen. Do you know how many people see a product or service on the market, and they say, "Ah! I had that idea! I should have done something about it!" Why didn't they? Because they feared failure. They didn't think about what could possibly go *right*; they thought about what could possibly go *wrong*. And that discouraged them from moving forward. And that is a shame.

The distinction of success, though, is the person who reaches past the rejections and failures of their lives.

The first 71 agents I approached with my first book, *Scratch Beginnings,* said, "Thanks, but no thanks." And then the 72nd said, "All right, let's do this."

Once my book was published, I spent many, many successive nights at the computer sending emails to journalists, editors, and producers to give me some coverage, to try to sell some books on the radio and online. Couple thousand rejections. And then a win.

When I was trying to play college basketball, I made contact with 138 college coaches. I assembled this database of coaches across the country, and I sent them emails, and I mailed them highlight tapes and game films, and I called them. I was a pain in the butt. And out of those 138 coaches, 137 of them told me they weren't interested. They rejected me. They told me to stop calling them.

But that 138th coach offered me a scholarship. 137 rejections. 1 acceptance.

Get. Back. Up. And. Get. On. The. Horse. Anybody can quit; anybody can walk away; anybody can make excuses. That's easy. That's weak. It's hard, though, *really* hard—and monumentally more rewarding—to fail and keep going; to make the decision, "Hey, I know that didn't work out like I planned it, but I'm going to figure out how it will."

There is a difference between someone who fails and someone who is a perpetual failure.

Do you know how many people I've met who have written books, who sent out 25 or 50 or 100 emails? They got rejected and then said, "Eh, well, I tried." You tried! 100 emails! This is your passion! And you're walking away after 100 emails? Not only did I get a couple THOUSAND rejections from producers and editors and journalists, some of them wrote to me with pretty negative commentary on what they thought about my story. What do you do? Send out 2001. Then 2002. Then 2003. Then 2004. You keep going. At some point, maybe it's time to redirect your energy and passion—maybe you realize that you're meant to do something else—but you can't do that after a few measly rejections, after you've invested five or ten hours. Muster all of your passion, throw your energy at it, get rejected, and adjust from there.

When I was in college, nineteen or twenty years old, my Pops said to me: "Keep failing. Sooner or later, one of your crazy ideas is going to pan out." And that's how I live my life. As long as I am continuing to move forward, each of my failures is one step closer to success.

Now, why is that? Why is it that each of our failures brings us one step closer to success? Simple. Because each of our failures, each of *your* failures, is an opportunity for you to take a look at what *isn't* working. Fighting through failure is good for the soul and shows that you represent persistence, and that is important. More importantly, however, each failure is an educational experience. After the satisfaction of working through failure, it is imperative to get busy recognizing *why* you failed. *Why* you were rejected. Because if you don't learn from these early errors, then you are doomed to repeat them later in life when there is much more at stake. I'm telling you: make as many mistakes as you can, as early as possible. Get them out of the way. Otherwise, if you close the door to failure you are closing the door to improvement, and you will then have *no chance* of moving forward.

And if you aren't able to determine precisely what went wrong, be quick to ask for feedback. What did I do wrong? Where can I improve? What can I do better next time? How can I avoid repeating this same rejection or failure? This runs in alignment with our first chapter on accountability. Own your successes, and own your failures. Don't be scared of them. Own them. I'm Adam Shepard, and I'm a failure. Say it with me. I'm Adam Shepard, and I'm a failure. Okay, now say it, and insert your own name. I'm _____, and I'm a failure.

"Why is it okay to fail?" you ask. Quite simply, someone who is struggling, someone who is fighting to succeed, is someone who is thinking outside the box, pushing to the edge. Anybody can take orders, follow them, and do exactly as they're told. Anybody can punch in, work the assembly line, and punch out at the end of the day. And there is definitely a time and place to follow the rules. But someone who is failing is challenging the status quo. They are acting within the law, but they are doing things a little differently; they are stepping outside the bounds of doing things as they've always been done.

And if you are venturing into the unknown—or at least something that is unknown to you—don't you think that failure is imminent? I'd say so.

You have to understand this about success: *everyone* says they want to be successful. Everyone has big dreams and big ideas and ambitious aspirations. And everyone, on the road to success, hits bumps in the road. And everyone is not prepared to confront those bumps in the road.

Success draws a line between those who fight through adversity and those who do not.

Of course there's a time to shift directions, to tackle a new project in your life. But that shift shouldn't come simply because you've failed. If you lose hunger for your pursuit or you have a better opportunity elsewhere...*those* are legitimate reasons to shift directions. Not failure, and most certainly not a series of rejection letters.

So, what do you do? Bet on success. Count on it. Plan on it. Every success story is the result of someone who fought through failure and rejection. Trudge forward, regardless of the adversity you've faced and the obstacles still lying ahead.

Let's consider one of the greatest presidents in the history of the United States. This dude failed in business at age 21. But he was undeterred. At 22, he lost a legislative race. But he kept going. At 24, he was busy failing in another business venture. But he told himself not to quit. His girlfriend died when he was 26, he had a nervous breakdown at 27, and he lost a congressional race at 34. So, he persisted. And he kept failing. He lost a bid for senate at the age of 45, and two years later he failed to be elected Vice President. Did he give up? No. He should have, though, right? He clearly is not cut out for greatness. But he didn't give up. He ran for senate again at age 49 and got beat. Again.

But then something crazy happened. He ran for president at age 52, and guess what. He won. That dude—the dude who lived through failure after failure after failure—became the leader of the most powerful country in the world.

Who was he? Abraham Lincoln. Here's a guy who could have given up, but he decided to battle against the odds, and now, you can find his face on two types of US currency, forever immortalized as one of the top leaders in U.S. History. Not so much of a failure now, is he?

And the list rolls on:

Steven Spielberg, the greatest movie director of all time, was rejected from film school THREE TIMES.

Harrison Ford, one of the greatest actors of all time, was fired from Columbia Pictures.

The Beatles were told that the trend for guitar music had passed.

Every. Failure. Teaches. You. Something. Every failure equips you with new knowledge, a new tool for your toolbox. And as I said, you are one day going to be able to look back and pinpoint those exact moments of failure that made you the inevitable success that you are going to become.

If you give up, then you are bowing to failure and rejection, and you are saying that you don't care to learn. Be curious. Be inquisitive. Read, ask questions, and observe the successes and failures of others. Surround yourself with successful people who were where you are now, who faced the same kind of difficulty that you are facing now. If you want to be an engineer, find an engineer in your town, and take them out to lunch. Ask them what they would do differently. You are going to fail plenty on your own—I promise you that—but maybe you can cut a little time off the learning curve if you can avoid the errors of others. Learn from their failures and successes just as you take time to learn from your own.

Now, let's go back to something I hinted at before: risk. Risk is *huge* when it comes to taking a look at what failure and rejection will mean for your ultimate fortune, good or bad. Risk is the dividing factor with failure, what separates the men from the boys and the women from the girls. Failure can often be associated directly with the risk that one assumes. They're essentially correlated. As one goes up, so does the other. More risk, more chance of failure.

But here's the thing: just as risk and FAILURE are correlated to each other, so, too, are risk and SUCCESS. The more risk you assume, two things are going to happen: you have a greater chance of falling on your butt *and* you have a greater chance to rise to the top. This risk of failure, though, as we've talked about, is a moot point, since you already understand that failure is going to happen, and the only thing you can plan for is the opportunity to learn and move forward.

So, that leaves success. More risk equals more failure, which equals more success. Studies show that riskier people are happier people. They have more satisfying lives and more satisfying relationships. Moreover, those who are risk-averse, those who shy away from making tough decisions, those who fear failure, are both less successful *and* less satisfied. Interesting, right?

Consider losing weight, for example. Losing weight involves a series of diet and workout routines. And every diet and workout routine doesn't work for everybody. So, what are you going to do if you work your way through a program that doesn't work for you? You try hard, and you don't lose any weight. Are you going to give up? No. You change the course a little. En route to finding out which diet works for you, you're going to find a host of diets that don't work. Remember Thomas Edison? He failed at inventing the light bulb 10,000 times before he got it right.

The Wright Brothers created many different ways not to fly, and then they soared through the air.

So, what does all of this boil down to? What does that mean regarding risk? It means that those who assume risk have a tougher road, but that road leads to a brighter end. Those who fail and get back in the game are ultimately successful. Life. Is. Risk. My question for you is whether or not you're going to make the choice to embrace failure now or in the future, when it could potentially be too late.

Take a risk. Fall on your face. And then get back up to take another one.

The great thing, and this is an important concluding point, is that you get to remember those days, the good ol' days of failure. These—*right now!*—these are the moments that make you appreciate success. You don't want everything to be smooth sailing. You don't want to just cruise through life and have everything handed to you. You don't learn anything that way. You don't learn how to think critically, make decisions on your own, and deal with the heated stress of a difficult situation. When you are blind to failure, you don't have a clue what it takes to succeed. You. Don't. Develop. As. A. Person. Until. You. Start. Dealing. With. The. Hiccups.

So what does that mean? Embrace failure. Embrace rejection. Love it. Learn from it. Get up and keep fighting. Because one day, you're going to look back, smile, and say, "Ah, look where I came from." You're going to appreciate that you had to *work* for your success. Other people's faith in you can wane, but the faith you have in yourself remains unshaken.

Ultimately, when all is said and done, you're going to love the challenge of failure, and you are going to love these moments of breaking through the tough times.

Workbook 3: Dealing with Rejection and Failure

Key points from this session:

- Adam Shepard has failed many times...
    - And so has EVERY successful person you know...
    - But they got back up and kept fighting.
- The same it is with your life: rejection happens. Failure happens. You are GOING to get rejected, and you are GOING to fail. The question then, is, "What are you going to do now?"
- Without the risk of failure, there is no opportunity for success. You've got to put something on the line if you expect to get something in return.
    - Don't think, "Something could go wrong."
    - Think, "When something goes wrong, I'll be prepared to fight through it."
- Persistence is the cure for any and all rejection.
    - Maybe, at some point, it is time to change gears, but not without giving a worthy fight.
- Each of your failures gives you an opportunity to see what ISN'T working, and therefore, you are able to learn from your mistakes.
- Learning from your mistakes is also a matter of asking for feedback from those around you.
- The initial stages are the most challenging. 80+ percent of small businesses fail because they don't stick through the initial tough times.

Leadoff question: How have your thoughts about failure and rejection changed since reading chapter 3? (And if they haven't, which is always a possibility, elaborate on the ONE biggest idea that you were able to take away?)

A look at your surroundings: Think about someone you know who has dealt with failure or rejection well. This could be someone who you know personally (a friend, a family member, a businessperson in your community) or it could be someone famous who you only know through the media.

Discuss a specific situation where they handled failure well. How did it turn out for them in the end?

3. Dealing with Rejection and Failure

A look back: Make a list of five (5) failures or rejections of your life. List a couple that were small and a couple that were larger and more significant.

1.

2.

3.

4.

5.

Learning from your past: Now, think about how you managed those failures or rejections. Did you take them in stride or could you have done something different to deal with these challenging times? List a couple of ideas of how you perhaps could have handled these specific situations better.

1.

2.

3.

4.

5.

Real world application: In the next two or three days, you are going to deal with a setback. Most likely, it will be small, but it will be a setback or a hindrance nonetheless. Will you handle it the same as you have before or will you make a different approach? REALLY be conscious of the way you've handled situations in the past and how much more success you could have if you handled this one another way.

Write about the situation below, and discuss how you handled it differently than situations in the past.

The next level: Failure is easier (although still a challenge) to deal with when you are fourteen, fifteen, or seventeen years old. When you're older, though, it gets tougher. Present a specific scenario on how handling the repercussions of failure has gotten more difficult as you have grown older.

How did you handle this situation differently than you might have when you were younger?

Four

Having the Courage to Be Different

I already know what you're thinking, that this is such a lame topic. "Yeah, yeah, yeah," you're thinking. "Be unique. I get it." But there's a lot more to it. Conformity is a huge issue in today's world. Huge. Big problem. For whatever reason, people's motives are all kinds of out of whack. We go in one of two directions: either we strive to be just *like* everybody else, just so we can fit in, or we make every effort to be exactly *opposite* of everybody else, just for the sake of showing off our uniqueness. Both are bogus and lazy and selfish. You shouldn't be worried about what others think. Who are they? The cool people? Do they make the rules? Listen, do you want to look back on your life and say, "I did everything just like everybody else did"? No. The answer to that question is "no".

Read the masters and listen to gurus and seek to emulate what has worked for those who have come before you and had great success? Indeed. But there is an outside-of-the-box component that cannot be dismissed.

I wouldn't be the person I am today if I wouldn't have understood the value in withstanding being different. I always saw my uniqueness as a flaw. I always wanted to fit in. But as I got older, I started to see that the people conforming to society—living lives in a mold or a bubble—weren't being productive; they weren't getting anything done; they weren't successful.

Once I saw the value in being different, I started to make things happen. This is when I started living great experiences, writing books, getting published, and finding sincere friendships. Of my four or five most sincere friendships in my life, we all share similar visions of success, and we all recognize the value in being different from one another.

Think about it: do you want to be remembered for being someone else? For being compared to someone else? Or for being someone else's sidekick?

Or do you want to carve your own name in the sand?

So, I challenge you to think about how you are different and how you can stand up to acknowledge the ways in which you're different; and more importantly what you can do to exploit how you are different. What distinguishes you? Your work ethic and the fact that you won't let anything or anyone get in the way of what you want to accomplish? Your passion? Your intellect? Your lack of interest in petty conversations or gossip? Your devotion to current, world issues? Your willingness to spend the weekend exploring the world through a book or a fun trip or a project rather than loafing around?

The great thing about all of this is that we are all, naturally, by definition, different. You have a unique race, culture, gender; your physical features are different from the next person, and your personality is different from the next person. Embrace this. Many people spend their lives trying to conform to society rather than appreciating their differences.

Being different doesn't mean showing off that you're different. It doesn't mean going out of your way to say, "Hey! Look at me! I'm unique! See?" Having the courage to be different means that you simply don't care what others think about you. You do your own thing. Maybe that works into the mission and vision of others, and maybe it doesn't. Sure, you'd like to collaborate with a group of friends on something, but if they aren't on board with you, then to heck with 'em. You've got a plan; you're on course. If you don't fit in just right with everybody else, that's fine. If you don't have the coolest new gadget or car or clothes that *everybody* else has, let me tell you something: you're going to be okay.

The reason I am the person I am today is because I'm different, because I've done things unconventionally. Do you remember everything I was telling you about my first book, about dealing with the rejections and failures? It took me 2500 emails to get one person to write up my story, but the lesson there is more than persistence. The lesson extends to doing things a little differently. From email 1 to 2500, I switched things up. I saw what was getting a response, what *was* working—basically, nothing—and I was open to change along the way. I did things differently. Other people weren't sitting at their computer typing emails to 2500 people. That's too hard. That's too irregular. They were trying more conventional means of getting to the media—email blasts that rarely get seen, for example—while I switched things up to be more personal.

And it worked. Being different worked for me. It started at a young age, kids making fun of my big, floppy ears—me recognizing that it is okay to be different—and it has continued into my professional life.

I am the person I am today, and I enjoyed the success I did with my first book, because I saw what was working for other people—I saw which email templates they were using, which marketing techniques they were using, which trigger words they were using—and I changed things up a bit. I made myself more distinctive.

Success comes to those who dare to be different. But that success doesn't come from these people being put in a position where they have the opportunity to be different. Nope. Success comes because they accept challenge from the beginning. They *put themselves* in a position to be different. They don't wait for the difference to come to them. They take it. As I noted earlier, they follow the rules, but they are always looking for ways to shake things up a bit.

I just saw a segment on CBS about this guy Ted Ginn, who never went to college but has founded a successful academy for troubled teens in Cleveland. It is one of the most successful public schools in Cleveland. It's amazing what he's been able to accomplish. When he was asked why it has been so successful, this is what he said: "I did so many things different. I did what other people didn't do...When everybody else is going right, I'm going left. Going right wasn't working. You gotta do something different."

He later went on to add about his school: "We want to be the best." And I'm telling you that in order to be the best. You've gotta be a little different.

So, I'm challenging you to think that maybe it's all right to answer questions a little differently once in a while. Say "no" every now and then. Say "yes" often. And then say "no" again. It's okay. You don't have to try to make everyone happy all of the time. That's unrealistic.

Now listen. I've heard the old adage "If it ain't broke, don't fix it" a thousand times in my life. Maybe two thousand. Maybe about a billion. That's a tired cliché. Somebody said it back in the 1400's, and that person didn't get much accomplished in his life other than being quoted, one time.

Colin Powell says that "'If it ain't broke, don't fix it' is the slogan of the complacent, the arrogant or the scared. It's an excuse for inaction, a call to non-arms." I love *that* quote. "If it ain't broke, don't fix it" is easy. You cannot be complacent, arrogant, or scared when making a decision. You can't be in inactive. If it ain't broke, you've got a solid foundation to build something better. Right? Maybe these changes are small or maybe they're dramatic, but the point is that you are always evolving, always changing, always developing. And that development starts by daring to be a little unusual.

The well-worn path is easy. It's not tough. It's been traveled before, so it must be okay to travel it again. If you take the well-traveled path, you don't have to do any work, any maintenance. There are no trees; you don't have to cut through bushes with a machete or pick weeds. Everything has already been laid out for you. You just, well, go. La di da.

The well-traveled path represents the attitude of the average. And you are not going to be average. You're going to be *great*, and on your rise to the top, you need to recognize that going with your heart is more difficult than going with your mind. Your mind thinks about what is rational, what makes sense. Your mind thinks about what it has the potential to accomplish.

Think about this for a second. Think about the most successful people and organizations in our world today and in years past. They reached the heights they did, because they did things a little different.

Galileo challenged conventional thinking, and as a result, he played a major role in the Scientific Revolution.

The Wright Brothers applied a unique perspective en route to the invention of the first airplane and their subsequent first flight.

David tried an unusual approach in his slaying of Goliath: a stone and a sling. Everybody else was trying the same tactics over and over or retreating altogether. David saw what wasn't working and tried a new approach.

Everyone you see on TV—from actors to athletes to musicians to news anchors—thinks of ways they can do things differently, establish themselves as unconventional.

Do you think Apple had a narrowly-focused vision when they came up with the iPad or the iPhone? How about Mark Zuckerberg and his invention of Facebook? You think he was stuck in a bubble world of doing everything like his fellow computer engineers? Nope. Everyone else was doing things one way, and he switched gears a notch or two.

Listen: every discovery, breakthrough, invention, championship team...every successful person you can name to me right now...they all had the courage to *be* and *think* different.

Follow the rules, always follow the rules, but think of ways to distinguish yourself. You weren't born to do what others do, what your friends do, or what society says you should do. You were born to do two things: find your passion and throw all of your effort into that passion until the day you retire and it's time to sit on the porch sipping lemonade. That is it. THAT. IS. IT.

Okay, I need to digress a little here, because, as I mentioned, I don't want you to think it isn't important to follow in the footsteps of those who have gone before you. Sometimes—and here is the great paradox—sometimes, you need to follow the leader. Just as it is okay to ask questions—Why, What, How—and it is okay to say "No" once in a while, it is also okay to say, "Yes." In certain situations, it can be okay to go with the crowd. Working as part of a team can be just as valuable as a quest undertaken alone.

Following in the footsteps of experts and paying attention to current trends can be important. You don't want to be different just for the sake of being different. That's stupid. Being different takes courage, but, in the right setting, it also takes courage and humility to keep your mouth shut and fall in line with the rest of the crew.

In many cases, it is important to work toward a common goal.

So, don't think that just because you're doing something different—"Look at me, Mom!"—

that you are going to enjoy success. It doesn't work like that. You've got to pick your battles. You've got to decide when and where to be different. Be strategic about it. Build on the success and wise words of the experts around you, your mentors. Do some things the same and some things differently.

What I'm trying to do here is challenge you to have the courage to be different, to think outside the box. Thinking outside the box will get you places, allow you to achieve your wildest dreams. Thinking outside the box will get you the shiny car, the big house, your dream job, extra free time, and a wonderful husband or wife. Thinking inside a bubble won't do that for you. Thinking inside the bubble will get you a car that constantly needs repair, a little house with a ten foot by ten foot room for you and your mediocre spouse, and the opportunity to work extra hours at a job that you don't really love.

Thinking outside the box means greatness. Thinking inside the bubble means mediocrity. I challenge you to get up and get serious about being great.

Critical thinking here is crucial. Critical thinking is the reason we've stepped beyond having to circle around a campfire for heat. Right? I mean, one day, about a thousand years ago, a little hairy caveman—we'll call him Bert—was walking around, and he was sick of having to build a fire every time he was cold, so, he invented a wood stove. And then his brother Frank said, "I'll do you one better," and he invented a heater. And then their cousin Jose said, "You guys are a couple of idiots." And he ran off to invent central heating, so that everyone could just flip a switch and be warm. They became a very wealthy family, what, with the invention of modern heating and all, but that's not what I'm getting at here. The takeaway is that their ability to look at a situation, and say, "That's good, but I can do better if I change things up a bit," is why we have advanced with heating.

Of course I might have my facts a little mixed up on how central heating was invented, but the point is that critical thinking is what advances our culture from one period to the next. From the rotary phone to the cordless phone, from the cell phone to the iPod, and from the smartphone to whatever kind of crazy technological machinery you have in your pocket now.

Conformity keeps us in one place. And conformity is what you've been taught.

And that's a bummer, because conformity is the devil of success. I love people who think differently and act differently. They inspire me. And they should inspire you. If you choose to think in a different way, you are choosing success. You *will* be successful. I'm not just making an empty promise here. I am *guaranteeing* you that if you choose to think differently you *will* maximize your potential. Guaranteed. You are choosing victory when you choose to be different.

Maybe you succeed right off the bat, but probably not. Maybe it takes you one, or two, or ten, or fifty times to get where you want to get. That's fine. As long as you're moving forward. Take someone else's approach and switch it up a little bit until you've got the result you want.

There's no point reinventing the wheel, right?

Besides, big opportunities don't come to those who follow a preset course. A preset course gets you mediocre opportunities and mediocre outcomes. Mediocre products. Mediocre services. A mediocre husband or wife. A mediocre house. And one day, mediocre kids. You. Will. Not. Have. Mediocre. Don't stand for it! You don't want to be number three or number four or number ten. You want to be number one. And number one comes from the big chances you get from being unconventional.

Think big, and act big. And You. Will. Get. Big. Chances.

You want money? Think big and act different.

You want to make the varsity team? Think big and act different.

You want to go on a date with that lovely girl or handsome guy that everyone has a crush on? Think big and act different.

I'm not just blowing smoke to make you feel good about yourself. The simple fact is that you are really *awful* at something. And conversely, you are *amazing* at something. I don't know what that is. Maybe it's the cello. Maybe it's football. Maybe it's math. Maybe it's writing. Maybe it's making bead necklaces and marketing them to sweet little old ladies at the local nursing home.

I don't know. But *you* know. Don't worry about what everybody else is good at and don't worry about cool new trends. Recognize them, and build on them. Create your own cool trend. I'm counting on you to do this, the world is counting on you to do this, and YOU should be counting on you to do this.

In the end, maybe you make lots of money and become one of the top players in your sport and date the most fantastic person in your school. Or maybe not. But I can assure you that acting like everyone else most assuredly won't get you there.

Dare. To. Have. The. Courage. To. Be. Different.

Workbook 4: Having the Courage to Be Different

Key points from this session:

- We are all different, in one way or another. Everyone has unique features, everyone has a unique personality, and everyone has a unique manner of handling their daily dealings.
- Being different doesn't mean *showing off* that you're different. It means acknowledging your differences, and figuring out how you can capitalize on those differences.
- Surround yourself with unique people who will help you move in the positive direction which you would like to go.
  - Learn from the unique, successful people around you—in the media and in your community.
  - Learn what you can from them and build upon it to create your own success.
- Always go with your gut instinct.
  - Being different will take you to the next level.
  - Being the same as everyone else will keep you right in line with them.
- Think critically.
  - Think different.
  - Be different.
  - Achieve amazing things.

Leadoff question: What is the ONE big thing you learned from this session? What is your big takeaway? (This can be a story, a lesson, a tactic, a call to action, or, well, anything.) Spend a paragraph or so elaborating on what this meant SPECIFICALLY to you:

Analyzing your hero: It is often easy to analyze what is different or unique about the people around us. Take a moment to consider your hero. Maybe he or she is an athlete, a politician, an author, an actor, or maybe it is someone from your hometown who is relatively unknown. Maybe they are still living or maybe they are an historical figure.

Below, discuss a few characteristics that are unique about them, that set them apart from those who DIDN'T make it to their level, who DIDN'T enjoy success. Maybe they have unique personality characteristics (their sense of humor), or maybe it is their attitude (their grit or sheer will to win).

4. Having the Courage to Be Different

The real you: Everyone wants to fit in, but it's nice to create our own path once in a while, right? We want friends and we want to be loved, but we also want to distinguish ourselves as ahead of the pack.

List 5 things (blending good and bad) that are different about you, traits that aren't necessarily represented by your peers.

1.

2.

3.

4.

5.

Now, one by one, follow that list up with the 5 ways that those differences can be exploited to your advantage. (And yes, no matter what your unique feature might be, it can be used to your advantage.)

1.

2.

3.

4.

5.

Session four activity: Do something out of the ordinary for someone. One thing, first chance you get. For example: you're a server at a breakfast joint. One of your customers asks you for a newspaper, but the restaurant doesn't supply them. You can say, "Well, sorry," or you can run around the corner to the gas station and pick up a copy. It will cost you a dollar and it will make his day.

Discuss below what your activity was, and how that impacted you:

Onward: You don't have to TRY to be different, but always appreciate HOW you are a different and WHAT you can do to capitalize on those differences.

And the same it is with those around us. They aren't "strange" or "outcasts" just because they are different. Take a moment to write about one person who you will try to learn more about (by taking them out to lunch, for example) despite the fact that many people consider them "different."

Five

The Importance of Organization, Rituals, and Habits

All of these various ideas on accountability and finding purpose and dealing with rejection are falling into place, but there are times that you simply feel disorganized, and that can put you in a rut. The things we're learning on purpose, failure, and accountability can easily lose traction if you lack organization and if you haven't established a few ritualistic practices. After all, these habits can keep you going in times of turmoil and then motivate you to fight through. You can count on these habits. You can count on an organized world around you. So many things you can't count on in this world—whether or not the bus will arrive on time, how your teachers will treat you, whether your boss will be nice or a pain in the behind—but you can always count on a morning ritual or having the world around you—your room, your locker, your car—organized to your liking.

I'll tell you why this is important to me. I have seen, personally, the developments you can have when you have an established regimen. My life was chaos when I was working through middle school and high school and even during the first couple years of college. I just didn't care. Didn't think about it. People said my life was a mess and disorganized, and I told them my life was organized in the way that *I* liked it. They didn't know where things were in my life, but I did. They didn't understand my tendencies and habits, but *I* did. Who are they to judge?

But it turns out they were right when they told me I needed more organization. Just as it is important to try different things, to switch it up, to always try something new, it is also important to have established trends. Repetition *can* be important, if used correctly and as a complement to the other areas of your life where you are constantly trying new things, constantly striving to do more and better. Genius doesn't happen if you are trying *everything* different or *everything* the same. You've got to keep it mixed up...some things stay consistent and some things change.

Consistency. Man, I'll tell you that consistency is key. Just as you want to be counted on to be passionate and to bring different ideas to the table—this is a very worthy reputation to have—you *don't* want to be erratic. Being distinctive is great; being all over the place is not.

This is an important idea to consider, because there is a fine line between consistency and unreliability.

Unique: good. Unstable: bad.

Extraordinary: good. Volatile: bad.

Weird: can be good. Reckless, though, is bad.

Now, how does this consistency relate to your daily habits?

Consistency means habit. Habit means repetition. And repetition becomes the fabric of who you are. Some things are good to change—as I said, if it ain't broke, make it better—but some things are good just the way they are. Some things don't need to be changed, they can't get better, and they won't get better. Reese's Peanut Butter Cups? Perfect...no need to change 'em. Asparagus? Perfect, no need to add any kind of hormones or fertilizers or whatever they add to make cows and plants meatier and greener. Some things are already where they need to be. Which is fine. And the same holds true for your daily actions. Some things are custom-built for you to get done and move along. Stay the course. Check it off the to do list, and go about busying yourself with something that you do have the power to change, something that *isn't* as routine.

More importantly, by keeping these things consistent, you are establishing a basis for advancement. If you have a ritual, for example, you feel a sense of accomplishment, like you've done something important, when really you've done little more than what you did yesterday and the day before that.

What do I mean by this? What on Earth am I talking about? Okay, let's consider, for example, your morning routine. Do you understand the value that your morning routine establishes for the balance of the day? In the morning, you set the precedent for everything else that is going to happen until you put your head on your pillow at night. Touching your feet to the carpet—or hardwood—next to your bed is the starting gun for your day's race.

So, consider the value that your morning routine has. The number one thing is to make your bed and clean your room. First thing, every day. You'll feel organized already. The ritual of keeping your room tidy is a ritual that will *ensure* that you can easily organize the rest of your world around you. It doesn't make sense for me to simply say these things to you, so we'll investigate further with the workbook activities, but for now, take my word that if your room is tidy—if your bed is made, if your clothes are picked up, if all of those papers are filed away—the consistency of the rest of your life will follow suit.

Ritual. Routine. Even softball players will have a ritual before they step up to the plate. The next time you're watching a softball game, take a look. Some girls will do the *exact* same thing, *every* time.

One, two, three shuffles with the feet.

One, two, three sways of the bat.

One, two, three shrugs of the shoulder or twists of the head.

It's routine. It's a ritual. Why is this important? Rituals put our mind at ease. This is a hectic, frenzied world, and rituals bring us back down to Earth. They put us at a good place. Rituals provide us with a sense of security, stability, and connectedness. They allow us to accomplish something without having to worry about thinking about it—like loosening up before hitting a softball, for example. Softball players can prepare for their at-bat physically with a ritual while mentally preparing how they want to handle this particular pitcher or the specific scenario depending on how many runners are on base, for example. Their ritual is second-nature, since they've done it thousands of times. Their mental game is *not* second-nature and requires them to focus on this particular situation. If they didn't have this ritual, they would have to focus their energy on both the physical side—physically loosening up—*and* the mental side—surveying the specific situation. The lack of a ritual would take away from the batter's mental game.

The thing is that rituals remind us what is important while also providing a level of stability and continuity. Once we are through our rituals, once we are rolling, the rest of the day is *ours* for the taking. We are a steamrolling, coal-toting locomotive, and we have a deadline to meet. Get. Outta. My. Way. With rituals, there is no opportunity to procrastinate or put things off. Do it now, do it well, and then move along.

Rituals can also be a great transition from one step of commotion to the next. Your morning ritual is your transition from sleep to the day ahead. Your midday ritual is a transition from the morning to the afternoon. Your pre-class ritual is your transition from the fun time in the halls to getting serious for class. Your evening ritual is an opportunity to cool down.

In fact, I just read a study that said that family rituals—eating dinner together, going to the movies together, going to football games together…doing whatever together—these family rituals make people feel happier, better loved, and more strongly a part of families. Fascinating how that works.

Many things, by the way, can consistently improve while remaining routine. Consider your workout program, for example. If you are overweight—whether by thirty pounds or three pounds—it can be important to have a consistent workout regimen so that your body knows what it's getting into. Establishing a set schedule—working out Monday through Friday or just in the mornings—is not only good for your body, but it's good for your psyche: you grow to count on yourself to work through the routine and then move along with your life. You. Count. On. It. This is important. Your motivation runs on the adrenalin of getting stuff done, of thriving on achieving both the expected *and* the unexpected. Sometimes, you don't know what is going to happen. Other times, it's important to have an idea, to work through a set schedule. This will keep you going, up and running. In a time when some things are going right and some things are not going right, you can count on your routine.

Listen, everything can't be chaos; some things need to be predetermined. There is a balance here.

Organizing your life around you involves *all* components. What you'll notice is that organization encompasses every aspect of your life: your workout routine, your professional life, your personal life. Think about how this applies to you. From your email inbox to your room to the way that you arrange the schedule of your day to your diet to the way that you file papers and place books on the shelf...your organization is everywhere.

Most important to note here is that your organization carries from one area of your life to the next, and that organization can give you momentum. You can't fake organization. You are either organized or not. You either have your life in order or not. No pretending. But what you have to understand here—and this is the most important aspect of all of this talk of rituals, habits, and organization—what you have to understand is that the organization of your life is linked. And as one piece falls, the rest are more likely to tumble.

As an example: last Tuesday morning, I woke up, got out of bed, put my slippers on, and walked to the kitchen to fix a bowl of cereal. And the kitchen was a disaster. A war zone. Dishes in the sink, dishes out of the sink. A banana peel hanging off the side of the counter. And between the Foreman grill, tupperware, paper towels, a cutting board, a big jug of water, a rolling pin, salt and pepper shakers, and the mail, there wasn't much room for me to work with to make my bowl of cereal. So, do you know what I did? Did I clear everything? Did I wash the dishes? Did I make my bowl of cereal elsewhere?

Nope! None of the above. I went back in my room, crawled back into bed, and wasted an hour on the computer. Was it because I was being lazy that morning? Partly, yes. But the lack of organization in my apartment fueled my laziness. One fed on the other. I went into the kitchen and *immediately* lost motivation. I was on the fence of either having a great day, a get-out-of-my-way-I'm-taking-over-the-world kind of day, or a "blah" day, a whatever day. It could have gone either way. And as a result of my poor organization, my day quickly shifted to a "blah" day.

Think about this, though: What if I would have taken four minutes to clean the kitchen before I went to bed the night before? Or, failing that, what if I would have walked into the kitchen that morning and hastened into Super Clean Overdrive. In short order (four minutes!), I could have put the dishes in the dishwasher and the trash in the garbage can, and I could have reorganized the miscellaneous items scattered about. In four minutes, I could have changed my day. Instead, I just didn't feel like it. The mess depressed me, so I went to sit in my bed for an hour. What a lazy piece of waste I was.

This may seem like an extreme example to you. I mean, who adjusts their day based on the disorganization of their kitchen? You're right, this is but one minor little example, but this is serious. Don't discount it. If I can walk in the kitchen and be de-motivated by a few dishes, think about how more serious situations, how more profound disorganization can spoil a pursuit.

So, the question, then, is, "How do you organize?" And the answer is simple: however *you* want to organize. *Your* organization in *your* world is *your* responsibility. Nobody else's. So, your friend Suzie's organization might be the same as yours or it might contrast yours altogether. Understand that this is not an excuse for you to shuffle your life into disarray and say, "Oh, no, but you don't understand. This is how *my* life is best organized." With clothes scattered on the floor and papers disheveled around your dresser and desk, you can't say, "Oh, I know where everything is! Don't worry." It doesn't work like that. If. Your. Life. Is. In. Disarray. You. Will. Not. Maximize. Your. Potential. It's that simple. Just as there is a case for everyone having their own organization, there is a standard that must be set.

I will say this, though: one way that you can organize your time is in increments…15 minutes, 30 minutes, an hour…whatever. This does several things: for one, it allows you to cram as much work into a short period of time as possible. This is maximizing potential. When you have a definitive end, it is easy to be more focused. "Okay, I have 45 minutes to accomplish this task. I need to get after it, and then I'll have a chance to relax." You have a direction, you have a goal, you have a defined endpoint. Think about it: we have a very short attention span anyway, and this can get us into trouble, particularly with major tasks that simply appear daunting. Put everything you can into that short bit—or long bit, whichever it may be—and then take time for yourself, to unwind.

I do this *all* the time…when I'm working out, when I'm cleaning the house, when I'm washing the car, moving furniture…everything. When I'm writing a book, I will sit down and say, "Okay, dude, you are going to write 300 words, and then you can have a treat." It's like I'm a pet and I'm rewarding myself for rolling over. But it works. I organize my morning or afternoon or evening or even the whole day into short bursts of excellence, rather than a drawn out day of mediocrity. And I get *much* more accomplished this way and the work I produce is *much* more quality. I mean, think about it: do you think it would be more effective for me to produce 300 quality words or 500 mediocre words? The answer is simple: 300 quality words, every time.

Your. Organization. Will. Allow. You. To. Produce. More. Quality. Results. This is a fact.

The other thing that bursts of time allow you to do is reel back and evaluate what is going on in your life. Take account. If you're just going, going, going, going at this frantic pace—without a break—you're much less likely to be able to see what you're doing right and wrong. Work hard for a spell and then...step back. Take a moment to look at the bigger picture. There's a saying—"work hard, play hard"—and that works in precisely with these ideas about organization.

Go out, handle your business, and prepare yourself to relax on the back end.

As I hope you've been able to see, rituals, habits, and organization all work together, hand-in-hand. Your rituals dictate your ability to prepare for the next event of your life, whether that event is five minutes long or five hours long. And your organization within that event—whether it is cleaning your room, arranging a very important meeting, or deciding homework priority for various subjects—is oh-so-important.

And your habits, in turn, are a representation of *everything* put together. Your habits dictate the person you are *now* and the person that you will become *later*. That's a simple, yet powerful statement. Your. Habits. Dictate. The. Person. You. Are. Now. And. The. Person. You. Will. Become. Later. Develop bad habits, and it will be a little bit of a struggle for you. Develop good habits, and there is unlimited opportunity for you to maximize your potential, whatever that potential may be.

I know this makes sense, because I've stolen all of this information from the people around me as I've grown older. I've read great books and surrounded myself with fantastic mentors, and from all of the successful people I've met in my life, the one constant in their lives is, in fact, consistency. They are sure to establish themselves as distinct from their competition, and they are quick to embrace change—as we'll talk about later—but *all* of the successful people I've met in my life have been able to do three things: establish great organization, perform steady rituals, and represent positive habits.

Workbook 5: The Importance of Organization, Rituals, and Habits

Key points from this session:

- There are many things you *can't* count on: who likes you; if your English teacher likes your writing; if your boss likes your work.
    - But you *can* always count on organizing your world around you: cleaning your room or performing your morning ritual for example.
    - And this organization can set you up to be incredibly efficient and do great things.
- A ritual or habit or routine means consistency. You can build on top of the consistency of your life.
    - You can take risks and...
    - change what isn't working.
- Your morning routine *might* be the most important part of your day.
    - From there, you are feeling good and riding that momentum into the rest of the day.
    - If your room is clean (bed made, clothes picked up, etc.), the organization of the rest of your life will follow suit.
- Having routine parts of our lives allows us to reenergize AND refocus without much mental exertion.
- You can make *monumental* changes with a consistent routine. (Consider your physical well-being, for example: a consistent healthy diet and a consistent workout routine can work wonders.)
- Consider working in bursts of time (45 minutes of work; 15 minutes of relaxation) in order to boost efficiency.

Leadoff question: Developing consistent habits and organizing your life around you is more difficult than it sounds. There is a lot of complexity to figuring out a simple routine (even if it's unproductive to spend a lot of time worrying about what your routine is going to be).

That said, take a moment to elaborate on the biggest lesson you were able to take away from this chapter?

And a quick follow-up: In addition to the one lesson you were able to take away, what struck you as a positive change you can make immediately (as in, RIGHT NOW) to your daily habits or rituals? Surely, something hit you while you were reading...What was it?

5. The Importance of Organization, Rituals, and Habits

Your life in disarray: Tomorrow morning, when you wake up, don't follow a routine. Don't make your bed, don't organize your room, don't follow a 1-2-3 step schedule. As a matter of fact, with the exception of places you have to be (school! work!), don't follow a routine at all. Do everything different than you would normally do it and without worrying about being efficient.

And back to organized: Now, switch it back to an efficient system of organization. When you wake up in the morning, be particular about your rituals: make your bed and follow a set schedule. In the evening, be conscious of a balance between "work time" and "play time" (work hard for 45 minutes and take a break for 15 minutes, for example).

Discuss below what kind of difference (if any) this makes on the rest of your day and on your productivity. If nothing else, did you hit the ground running in the morning with a little more momentum? Did you feel more efficient with your work/play schedule?

Calling back to the chapter: In the session, you heard about the pregame rituals of various athletes, from basketball players to football players to softball players.

Talk for a moment about your own "pregame" ritual (for a sport or band practice or even preparing to do homework or take a test). How does this affect your performance? Is there anything you feel you can (or need) to add to your pregame ritual or are you happy with it as it is?

Moving forward from here: Your routine can always evolve and adapt to your current lifestyle and the world around you. Consider your morning routine this morning, for example. Discuss one thing you can do differently *tomorrow* to make your morning routine more efficient than it was *today*.

Six

Problem Solving

There are a lot of components to problem solving, some of which extend from the other lessons we're going through in the other sections, and some that are going to be new. The most important component of problem solving—THE. MOST. IMPORTANT. COMPONENT. OF. PROBLEM. SOLVING.—is to think win-win. That should be your goal, *every* time. Think about how you can get the most victories out of one situation, how everyone can maximize what they'd like to get out of a negotiation. If it's two people, you want it to be win-win. If it's three people, you want it to be win-win-win. If it's fifty people, you want it to be win-win-win-win...you get the idea. You want to maximize winning. That is your goal. The end result can, indeed, be that everyone wins, or at least that everyone is appeased. After all, that's the best attitude to have, but isn't it kind of the *only* attitude to have? Think about it: How much sense does it make to go into a situation where compromise is possible and think, "I'm going to get everything I can; I'm going to take everything I can; and I hope the other person gets nothing." That's shouldn't be your motive when problem solving.

Now, before we get too far, I'm telling you to think win-win, but you should also understand that it doesn't work like that every time. Everybody is not *always* going to get *everything* that they want. Your attitude beforehand should definitely be that you want to maximize each party's options, but you also don't want to spend outrageous amounts of time under the delusion that you are looking for an optimal solution. I understand that you have to protect yourself. Sometimes, an optimal solution might mean that someone has to give up more than they'd like to give up. Be mindful of this. This isn't ideal, obviously, but in some situations, it's much more realistic. Shoot for the win-win, and understand that you might have to stop short of that.

So, what role do you play in the process of problem solving, of compromising, of shooting for this win-win situation? You need to consistently think: Is it that serious? Can I concede this point? Am I willing to give a little here? What am I willing to give? What can I *give* so that I *get* what I want so that both parties will be satisfied?

The thing is to always think, "What can *I* be doing to solve this problem?" The bottom line is that you can't control what others are doing, but you can control your own actions, your own ability to reach a happy negotiation. You don't know what the other person is thinking, and you don't get to make their decisions for them. It's that simple. But you monitor your role in a confrontation. "Here's a problem. Now what can *I* do to help us reach a conclusion?" After all, you are you, and you can only control you.

Listen, what I'm telling you pretty much goes against almost everything else I'm trying to teach you regarding winning. Yes, you need to have a barbarian's instinct. Yes, you should want to win in life. Yes, you should want to have the mentality to be the greatest. But sometimes, as we'll talk about in our final chapter, you have to step back and be humble.

Hey, you want to win? You want to be tough? Yes, you do. But you can be compassionate and nice and have friends and still be tough. And your toughness can extend to problem solving. But just know that it's not necessarily tough to go after someone, to challenge them, to retaliate. It's not tough to be defensive. It's tough to take a step back. It's tough to give something up even if you *know* that is the best solution.

You will have to do this from time to time. You will have to give something up. You will have to have compassion for the other side. You have to give a little.

And this is okay.

After all, if you *don't* do this, you obviously run the risk of not reaching a resolution at all. And with no resolution, nobody wins, right? Nobody gets what they want. So there comes a time that you might have to give in a little—or maybe a lot—and that's fine. Ask yourself if it's really that important. Ask yourself if, in the long run, it's really going to matter. Maybe, but probably not. You're going to miss a television show every now and then; you're going to miss chances to hang out with your friends every now and then; on occasion, your job will need you to work longer hours. This happens. Deal with it. Give a little. In the grand scheme of life, it's not really that serious *and* most importantly, every time you concede a point or arrangement, you are developing your reputation as someone who is willing to compromise.

Now, if there's *one thing* that can make an ENORMOUS difference in your problem solving techniques, that one thing is *tone*. The tone of your voice can be the difference between a reasonable negotiation and an argument that quickly gets out of hand. I'm telling you: a calm tone is taken seriously and will get results; an escalated tone will get you nowhere, and fast. You want to be taken seriously, and your tone of voice is what will enable that to happen.

Let's use a simple, hypothetical situation at your house. Let's say, for example, that you're watching your favorite show on TV, and your fiancée comes in to tell you that it's time to mow the lawn. Now, she's already asked you four times this week to do it, and for whatever reason, you neglected to do so. But here you are: lawn needs mowing; your favorite show is on. You say, annoyed, "Yeah, yeah, I'll get to it after this show," and you dismiss her.

Now, your fiancée gets a little feisty. This isn't going to work for her. "I done asked you four times to go out and cut that grass! You best get off yo be-hind and get goin'." If your fiancée is ninety-three and from my home state of North Carolina, that might be how she sounds.

It seems, though, that everybody is losing in this situation. At the very least, *somebody* is going to lose, right? Either you are going to miss your favorite show or the lawn is not going to get cut. One or the other is most assuredly going to happen. And there's a lot of frustration in the air. Fiancée wants the lawn mowed; you want to watch your show. Nobody is willing to budge. To make things more volatile, anger is growing in your fiancée's voice, and this is making you fight back with contempt. This ain't lookin' pretty.

This is a typical situation that can quickly grow out of hand. All major problems start as a minor problem, and this is a minor problem that can blow up. And if it grows out of hand, truly, no one is going to get what they want.

- But there is one way for you to work out of this situation. What if you muted the TV for 30 seconds, lowered your voice to a calm, rational tone, and said this:

"Okay, babe. Listen. I know that you have been telling me to cut the grass all week. And for whatever reason—mostly laziness—I have neglected to do so. I'm a bad person, and I'm sorry. But I *really* want to watch this show. You know it's my favorite. I haven't missed a single episode this whole season. So, do you think it's fair if we make a deal: As soon as this episode is over, I will immediately go out and start the mower. I won't eat, I won't check my email...if I have to go to the bathroom, I won't go. I will *immediately* go cut the grass. What do ya say?"

Now, do you see what happened there? For one, you used a rational tone, and a rational tone will get you places when you're trying to solve problems. Two, you were self-effacing. You took accountability for being lazy, and by acknowledging that you should have cut the grass sooner, she now takes you more serious when you speak to her as an adult rather than saying, "Aw, golly dang honey. I'll cut the grass tomorrow. Leave me alone, woman!" Most importantly, you offered a reasonable solution, with which you can both win: you get to watch your show and the grass will be cut within the next hour.

Now, both of you are giving something up here. You're losing thirty valuable seconds of your favorite show in order to present your appeal to her, and your fiancée is going to have to watch the grass grow for another thirty minutes. Theoretically, you are both giving something up, but it's a minor something, and in the grand scheme of things, it doesn't matter.

Compromise. That's what this is about. This is win-win. You're both giving something up, but you're both winning big.

And most importantly, this minor problem doesn't blow up into something bigger.

Now, maybe your fiancée says, "No." In which case, you just need to take your loss, turn off your show, get your butt up, and go cut the grass. And you should do it, without argument, if your fiancée is unwilling to budge. You should have cut the grass earlier in the week when she first told you to go out and do it. But it's also worth giving it a shot, to peacefully ask her if it's reasonable to wait another thirty minutes. In fact, it's quite conceivable that this will make your fiancée have a new level of respect for you. She'll take you more serious if you use a rational tone. And next time she asks you to cut the grass, you can do it *first thing*, and save your tone of compromise for when you can really use it.

Moving forward, the idea is that you will become such a good problem solver that you will be able to solve simple problems automatically, making room for the more complex problems that arise. And it starts with compromising with your fiancée about when to cut the grass, and it extends to which markets your company will expand into or how to allocate various Research and Development funds. I mean, quite simply, life *is* problem solving, and the better you can solve problems, the more free time you will have to enjoy life. If your life becomes 80% problem solving, you'll never have a smile on your face, but if your life is comprised of a small percentage of problem solving, issues you're able resolve sooner than later, you'll be happier, more successful, and more fun to be around. You can hang your hat on that.

Okay, so after all of this talk, the question then is *how* do you go about solving problems. What is the process, the formula? I've presented some general techniques here already regarding style and tone, and I hesitate to offer a tangible, defined method of problem solving. Everyone's technique is going to be different. That said, four steps you must adhere to are: define the problem; establish your goal or desired end result; generate possible solutions; and present and decide on a solution. Simple: define the problem; establish your goal or desired end result; generate possible solutions; and present and decide on a solution.

That sounds like a lot when I say it altogether, but it's actually not that hard: the trick is to make sure you have a clear definition of the problem, know where you're going, and get there. As I said before, always be solution-oriented. "What am I doing to make sure that we are working forward toward a solution?" Then you present possible solutions, and work with all parties— yourself included—to make sure everyone is satisfied. Think about how the problem affects you, personally, and then step out to think about how the problem—and proposed solutions—might affect the other parties involved. Don't be greedy! Be humble. Goodness gracious. I'm repeating myself here, because *everybody*, when it comes to trying to reach a resolution, thinks about how *I'm* affected, how this applies to *me*. What this is going to mean for *my* day, *my* future, *my* life. Which is great. You should absolutely be concerned about how this affects you, but you should also have your mind on how this will affect others. This is a *crucial* key to the problem solving process. "How will this affect me?" And, "How will this affect others?"

A final step to the problem solving process, then, is perhaps the most important one: analyzing the solution. Think about it: if you don't learn anything from solving a problem, then it's likely that the problem is doomed to repeat itself. If, for example, after you have resolved the lawn mowing problem with your fiancée, and she *continues* to have to ask you four flippin' times to mow the lawn in the future, then you've clearly learned nothing from this process of problem solving. It doesn't matter what kind of tone or style or method you use, if you are not learning from your mistakes—if you are not learning from your previously solved problems—then you are not moving forward. You are doomed to see the same problems over and over again. The way you remove yourself from seeing the same problems over and over and over again is by seeing these problems before they even happen. And the way you see problems before they even happen is by evaluating the solutions to your past problems.

Analyze. The. Effectiveness. Of. Your. Solution. And protect yourself from having to deal with the same problems repeatedly.

See, at some point, you're going to come to realize that some problems are not solved fairly. "Oh, boohoo, and deary me, that just wasn't fair." Calm down. Life isn't fair, Champ. Get used to it. Not only are you not going to win every argument; not only are you not going to get what you want in every situation; not only are you going to walk away at times wishing you could have gotten a little more from a resolution. More than *all* of that, let me tell you something: there are going to be times that you are absolutely going to lose. You are going to get the short end of the stick. You're going to get hammered. You're going to get shafted. Pick your own analogy or metaphor or cliché. Not only are you going to have to give up something every now and then, at times you're going to have things taken from you in the bargain. It's gonna happen. I can promise you that. And the way you react to these situations, the way you react to these moments when problem solving just doesn't go your way, is the foundation for your character. When you lose, and react with class, you are immediately proving that you are better than the problem or the solution, and you are proving that you are resilient and can withstand very nearly *any* situation.

Workbook 6: Problem Solving

Key points from this session:

- It is vital that you learn how to solve problems NOW as opposed to LATER in your life. This can give you a huge leg up against your peers.
- Problems are never solved "fairly", but the most important component of problem solving is to think win-win. Think about how as many of the parties as possible can get as much as they want. Try to compromise.
- Compromise, though, might be a matter of giving up something that you really want. Ask yourself if it's really that important (because in the grand scheme of things, it's usually more important to go ahead and solve the problem).
- The tone of your voice can make a *huge* difference in your ability to solve problems. A calm tone will be taken more seriously and will get better results.
- The four key steps to problem solving are:
    1. Define the problem.
    2. Establish your goal or desired end result.
    3. Generate possible solutions.
    4. Present and decide on a solution.
- Then, analyze the solution and consider how you can more effectively solve the problem later.

6. Problem Solving

Leadoff question: With the ability to solve problems effectively as part of your toolbox, you will have a distinct advantage over your peers and your competition. But this takes practice, right?

Leading off, discuss the ONE biggest lesson (or tactic or story) that you are able to take away from this session. What, in particular, resonated with you?

Looking back, moving forward: We all have problems. Regardless of our wealth or standing in life, problems always present themselves. Big problems; small problems; and everything in between. The question is not: "Can I get through this day without any problems?" The question is: "How will I react when a problem does strike?"

Think of a problem that you solved recently (within the last week) where you didn't get your desired result. How could you have handled it differently in order to get what you wanted? What will you do differently next time?

Taking action: So, today is a new day. With new problems. And new opportunities to solve those problems.

Today, when a new problem presents itself (large or small), consciously use the problem solving steps you learned in this session (define the problem; establish your desired end result; generate possible solutions; decide on a solution) to solve it. Remember that your tone of voice is a *huge* determinant of your ability to compromise with someone.

And remember to think win-win regardless if this problem is with someone you like or dislike.

Discuss below the details of the problem and how you went about handling that problem.

The next step: Now, look forward to a much bigger problem that you could potentially have to face when you are thirty, forty, or fifty years old. Talk about how you might use the tactics you used in the previous example (a smaller, more current problem) with this much bigger future problem.

Moving forward from here: As talked about in the chapter, the key to solving many problems is to neutralize them before they strike.

Consider (and discuss below) one way that you are going to neutralize a problem before it strikes, starting this week.

❦

Seven

Living with Enthusiasm and Passion

❦

Let me ask you this question: What would you do if you knew that this was your last day on Earth?

I mean, if you were somehow able to determine that this was your last day on Earth...what would you do? How would you live your life?

How about if this was your last week on Earth?

Or your last year? The doctor says, "Uh, yeah, see, uh, the, uh, problem is this big black thing here. I'm not exactly sure what it is, but it ain't good. I'd say you got about a year left on this side of the dirt. Uh, yeah. Dat ain't good, but, uh, best wishes to ya." The first thing you would probably do is get a second opinion. But then, if the first doctor's prognosis was confirmed, what would you do? Would you live your life differently than you are living it now? Or would you stay on course?

This is an interesting question, a purely hypothetical one, for sure, but let's consider for a moment that hypothetical scenarios are the fabric of both our imagination, how the reality meets the road, so to speak. Just for fun, consider: what would we do? Right? What would you do if you had a definitive deadline?

I mean, seriously, who doesn't enjoy a good game of *Would You Rather?* in the car on a long road trip with the family? Besides, who knows when it could come to fruition that you might have to decide between breaking up with your significant other in a smelly port-a-potty or in front of a million people? And it's fun to know if you would rather have the ability to fly or to read people's minds. And if it comes down to it, I want everyone to know that I would rather kiss a beaver than get stung by a bee.

But the thing about hypothetical questions is that they give a view into our thoughts, our feelings, our emotions, our goals, our dreams, and our visions. They offer a gut-check on reality. Hypothetical questions set the standard for who we are...what we would do if in a certain situation. I want you to know that I've got your back, and I want to know that when the time comes, you and I are on the same page, that we would more than likely act in the same manner. So, when I ask you, "Would you rather spend the rest of your life with the person of your dreams living in a tent OR *never* find the person of your dreams but magically find two hundred dollars in your pocket every day for the rest of your life?" I get a perspective on who you are as a person. Your values stand out. Do you value money and your career, or do you value relationships?

This is why hypothetical questions can be important.

And besides, this is entertainment, right? A peek into your personality.

So, go ahead, answer this: What would you do if you had one year left on this Earth, one year left to accomplish everything you'd like to accomplish. Your To Do list can't wait any longer. You've got to do it now. I'm asking you, if you had one year left on this Earth, what would you do?

Now, the bigger question, the question that we're going to work on answering today: what is it that is different about those days, those months, that year, than the life you are living now?

This is about living your life with passion, enthusiasm. About getting after it. About going at it with a smile, about taking failure in stride with a smile, and success in stride with a smile. You've got two choices: get after it, or not. It's that simple. And getting after it starts with a foundation of passion and enthusiasm.

I don't care if you have a lot of money, a little money, no money, or money growing out in your backyard from a money bush. I don't care what kind of friends you have, what kind of success you've enjoyed so far, what kind of family you come from, or what kind of crazy, unbelievable talents you have. I don't care if you just won the state championship or if you didn't win a game all season. I don't care if you can play the flute, the cello, the guitar, and the piano at the same time or if you can't play a CD in your parents' car. Even more, I don't care about those things moving forward in your life, tomorrow, next Thursday, in five years, in fifty years...if you are not living your life with passion, then you are not living your life with purpose. And if you are not living your life with purpose, as we've already discussed, your life is stuck in a rut. And it will continue to be. Until you get a little pick me up.

You. Are. Good. At. Something. And it's high time to find that something and pursue it with passion.

Now, I'm not talking about "Rah, Rah, Sis, Boom, Ba", LETS-GO-GET-EM-COACH kind of passion. That's superficial passion. I'm talking about tangible passion. This is not *talk*-about-it passion. This is *be*-about-it passion. This is mustering all of your energy in pursuit of one thing.

I'm talking about living, breathing, drinking, and eating with your dream on your mind, and snuggling up next to it when you go to bed at night. I'm talking about pursuing it with everything you've got.

I'll tell you about a man who lives with passion. Dick Hoyt lives with passion. Have you heard of this guy? He is pretty amazing. If you've never heard of him, you should go Google him or watch a video on YouTube. Dick Hoyt.

His son, Rick, was born with cerebral palsy after the umbilical cord was wrapped around his neck. This cut off the oxygen from getting to his brain, and his brain has thenceforth been unable to communicate with his muscles. Now, he basically has no control of any function below his neck.

The doctor told Dick to institutionalize his son, that he'd be a vegetable for the rest of his life, that he'll never understand the world around him. Dick said, "I don't believe you. I don't believe that's true. Tell him a joke." So, the doctor told Dick's son a joke, and he laughed. Dick marched out of that doctor's office and found another doctor.

So Dick and his wife went about caring for their son. One day, Rick heard about a charity run for a paralyzed athlete, and he asked his father if he could push him. Dick said, "Yes."

Afterwards, Rick relayed to his dad through his specially-designed dictation machine what a fantastic time he'd had. He wrote: "Dad, when we're running, it feels like my disability disappears." And that's all Dick needed to hear. He immediately started training to run races. He created a three-wheeled buggy so that he could push his son as he ran. He tied a rope to a raft and pulled his son when he swam. He developed a special bike with a special seat in front of the handlebars, so his son could ride along as he biked. Together, they competed in many races—triathlons, marathons, 5Ks, ironmans. Do you know what an ironman triathlon is? That's a 2.4 mile swim, 112-mile bike, and a full marathon on foot. And here's a dude pushing, pulling, and carrying his son alongside other athletes who are competing unhindered.

That's passion.

Why does he do it? "Purely for the awesome feeling," he says, when he sees Rick's cantaloupe smile as they run, bike, and swim together.

That is passion. When he completed his first 5K with his son, Dick was hurting afterwards. Once he started training harder, though, he started kicking out unbelievable times. Like two hours, forty minutes, and forty seven seconds in the Boston Marathon. And an ironman triathlon in 13 hours, 43 minutes, 37 seconds.

That's crazy. That's unbelievable. I ran a marathon when I was 23, and I didn't break four hours. I ran a triathlon three weekends ago, and I decided halfway through that I didn't want to do another one. I barely finished. I just wanted a Gatorade and any free snacks I could get my hands on. I was literally walking in the pool to finish the swim. That's probably not legal.

Afterwards, I hurt for three days. I'm not a quitter, but I just learned that triathlons aren't for me. And that was a mere triathlon: a few mile run, ten mile bike, and a dozen or so laps in the pool. Forget an ironman triathlon; I was happy to complete this little mini sprint triathlon.

Dick, who used to be a self-described "porker" probably wasn't much for racing and competing either. But when he saw his son's eyes light up and a smile stretch across his face when they were competing together on the course, he knew that this is what he wanted to do. He wanted to compete with his son. His career in the military was merely a tool for him to be able to do what he really wanted to do: race on the weekends with his son. To date, they've competed over 1100 total events…240 triathlons, 6 ironmans, 68 marathons, 214 10Ks, and 22 duathlons. I don't even know what duathlon is, but it's probably hard.

This is crazy, don't ya think? This is unbelievable. And THIS. IS. PASSION. Passion means finding something—a hobby or profession—and maybe even someone you adore and putting every piece of your enthusiasm in that direction.

One of the biggest things that I'm able to take away from the story of Dick and Rick Hoyt is that passion and enthusiasm is about the journey. It's not about the end result. Dick doesn't *love* running and swimming and biking, but he loves running and swimming and biking *with his son*. Listen, I am very competitive, and I want to win more than anyone else. And when I lose—at anything, from a basketball game to ping pong to beating my roommate to the corner to get the mail—it bothers me. But to me, it's not about the end result. It's about putting everything you've got into something.

Do you know how many friends I have who are *miserable* in their day jobs? Miserable in their day-to-day lives? Miserable. They wake up and go to a job they don't love, and they come home lacking a project, a diversion, a leisure pursuit that they'd love to accelerate. I mean, where's the motivation? You need a passion. You need a project.

The key is what happens after your homework is done, after you get off work. What is your project, your passion? What are you *really* working on? What is your life's work? Maybe it aligns with your schoolwork or your day job, or maybe not. Maybe you're pursuing your dream as a musician or journalist or athlete or volunteer or martial artist or dancer or personal trainer or computer engineer…I mean, whatever. It doesn't matter. Sure, maybe it's evolving, but find something, and pursue it. Pursue it with passion. You have your job and you have your real interests. One day, those two worlds will collide, but in the meantime, you can be motivated by the passionate pursuit.

So, you're asking the question, searching for what you can be passionate about. "Shep," you're asking. "What is something that I can get enthusiastic about?"

And my response to your question is ANYTHING! My goodness…ANYTHING! SOMEthing…

ANYthing. Think about what you love, what you're good at. Maybe it's the same thing or maybe not. But pick something. And get after it. So many people spend so much time analyzing, "Okay, well I'm kind of good at this, and I'm okay at that, but I'm just not sure which to pick." And then people do a risk assessment and think about how much competition there is and how much time it could conceivably take away from other pursuits and "Oh, well, what if I'm not good at this?" and on and on and on. That's ridiculous. Too much. Pick something! Anything. You can easily talk yourself out of pursuing your passion. Don't over-think this. Just do it. It. Doesn't. Matter. What. Your. Passion. Is. Just pick one!

Now, maybe you're thinking, "What if I'm not sure what I'm passionate about?" That's fine, too! You shouldn't pick a passion just to have one. You can, however, be passionate just for the sake of being passionate. What I'm telling you is that by doing something—anything—you will discover your passion. Maybe you do it by deduction. Okay, I don't love that, and I don't love that, and I don't love that. Eventually, you will reduce your list down to what you do love.

Passion and enthusiasm start with a determination and a smile, and all of this radiates into one thing: energy. No-holds-barred-get-out-of-my-way-I'm-coming-atcha kinetic energy. Watch Out energy. Enthusiastic people radiate energy. Enthusiastic people get things done. Enthusiastic people love what they're doing, they show it, and they inspire other people to live life accordingly.

Think about the differences between the happy people and the unhappy people that you know. Are the unhappy people successful? Are they fun? Do they have that sprightly, infectious energy? Do *you* like spending time with unhappy people?

What about the happy people you know? Think about the friends and family and random people you know who exude happiness. They're more successful, aren't they? They have more energy and they are surrounded by more positive people, aren't they? Of course they are! Happy people are energetic, and happy people are successful. This is just how life works.

I mean, really, you have a choice in the morning. This isn't rocket science. When you wake up in the morning, you have the choice to either be A) happy and energetic, or B) sad and miserable. This isn't a decision that you allow others to dictate. Your passion and your energy are one of those things that you get to choose. Your parents are mad at you, your boyfriend just broke up with you, and you just got cut from the volleyball team. I mean, *that* is a miserable week. *And* you have homework assignments due tomorrow that you haven't started yet.

But check this out...so what! You still have the opportunity to choose how you'd like to tackle all of these issues. And passion and enthusiasm—and a smile—are going to get you through them with much more success than if you mope around. Seriously, this is a choice. And this choice—to live life with passion—will directly influence your successes and your failures.

Because listen, if Shakespeare said that all the world is a stage, then maybe what he meant is that the roles we play—the lives we *pretend* to lead—will inevitably become the lives that we *will* lead. So if we smile, we'll become happy. If we pursue with passion, we'll make things happen. Dale Carnegie said, "Act enthusiastic and you will be enthusiastic." Make sense?

Everything you do, do it all out, 100%, hold nothing back. If you screw up, screw up better than anyone else ever screwed up in the history of screwups. I'm serious. If you're going to screw up, make a mess; and then clean it up, and learn from your mess. Don't go 50% or 55% or even 90%. Go 100%.

I read an article recently, written by a physician, and he noted that his patients who attack life with passion heal their injuries quicker. Imagine that. He talks about two different kinds of people: the ones who come in with a smile and are ready to rehab and take care of their body; and the ones who come in and try to milk their injury, who have the philosophy to find what *other people* can do for them. This second person will milk his injury—try to get as many days off as he can, try to get as much free stuff as he can, try to get other people to help him—almost to the point that he *becomes* his injury. His injury begins to define him.

Wow. Think about that. So, not only does a passionate mindset affect us mentally, but it can affect our physical state as well. And this is a choice.

I'll leave you with this, before we move along to the workbook: Live today as if this is your last year on Earth; your last month on Earth; your last week on Earth; your last day on Earth. Take it one day at a time, one week at a time, one month at a time, and so on, and remember that, *If you change your demeanor today,* the rest of your life will change accordingly. And you can carry that with you forever.

Workbook 7: Living with Enthusiasm and Passion

Key points from this session:

- You have control over your passion.
    - You can get after it <u>or</u> not.
    - You can be happy and energetic <u>or</u> sad and miserable.
- Your income and your success don't matter if you are not living your life with passion.
- You can be passionate and enthusiastic about *anything*. Nobody is restricting you from what you're allowed to pursue (as long as it is safe and within the confines of the law). Just pick something!
- A smile is the first step to living your life with enthusiasm and passion: take everything with a smile. No, you don't want to be superficial, but you *can* be passionate *without* being superficial.
- Passion starts with determination and a smile and radiates into one thing: energy.
- Rather than being *good* at many things, focus on being *great* at one or two things.
- The key to living your life with passion is to do everything 100%.
    - If you are pursuing your dream, do it 100%.
    - If you screw up, make a complete 100% mess. And then clean it up.

7. Living with Enthusiasm and Passion

Leadoff question: What is the ONE big thing you learned from this session? What is your big takeaway? (This can be a story, a lesson, a tactic, a call to action, or, well, anything.) Spend a paragraph or so elaborating on what this meant SPECIFICALLY to you:

Evaluating your enthusiasm: Sometimes, it's easy to lose sight of just how much of a difference enthusiasm can make in our lives.

Consider one of your pursuits from the last week or so. This could be a game you played or a school project you were working on or a task you were performing around the house.

What role did enthusiasm play in your pursuit? Were you enthusiastic or not? Did you get the results you wanted? And most importantly, how could your experience have been better if you would have been a little more enthusiastic or passionate, if you would have had a bigger smile on your face? Or were you happy with the enthusiasm you represented?

The next year of your life: Keeping your income and restraints of time under consideration, list the five things you would do if this was your last year on Earth.

These can be realistic business pursuits, personal pursuits, academic pursuits, or vacations.

1.

2.

3.

4.

5.

Taking action on your passion: Now, list 5 reasons that you CAN make these 5 things happen. Keeping in mind your financial standing and the time that you have to commit to other pursuits, list 5 ways that you can make your five dreams a reality.

1.

2.

3.

4.

5.

7. Living with Enthusiasm and Passion

Session seven activity—smiling: There are *plenty* of ways to charm someone, but your tone and your disposition can mean that you are either inviting or uninviting.

The biggest aspect of your disposition is your smile. There's a statistic that says that 64% of people smile less than 20 times a day at home and 72% of people smile less than 20 times a day at work. That's craziness.

So, for the next two days, practice your smile. Smile at everyone, all day, everywhere. Don't be fake, but simply change your temperament. Discuss below how that affects your enthusiasm and your passion. Do you feel better? Do you feel more energized? Do you find momentum and get more done?

And most importantly, did your smile help you fight through more challenging times?

The Next Level: Being passionate and pursuing your purpose with enthusiasm are what can mark you as distinct from those who are simply cruising through life.

As you move forward, remain conscious of what it is that you represent (your purpose, and by extension, your passion), and be mindful of how you can continue to move forward, full steam ahead. After all, if you are not going 100%, you might as well go 0%, right?

Eight
Managing Your Work Ethic

Nobody can *make* you want to be a better person. That comes from you. That comes from within. It's simple: you either want to be successful or not. I don't care. Your neighbor doesn't care. The landscaper doesn't care. That funny-looking guy that nobody knows who constantly walks by your house doesn't care. Sure, your friends and your parents and your teachers and your coaches and your mentors and your boss and your coworkers...they "care", but at the same time, there is a limit to that. They care to the extent that you care. So, if you show a lack of interest in excelling, they will try to push you for a while, but after a few failed attempts, they will start to see that their energy is best spent elsewhere, particularly with someone who is willing to take initiative. Certainly, they have their own lives to worry about. They respect you but they can't be expected to stand over you with a wagging finger, telling you to buck up and get after it. That comes from you. You're not born with it. You don't buy it. It isn't handed to you. You don't walk down the street one day, and "Oh, hey! There's the fortitude and ambition and determination that has been eluding me. Where have you been? I've been looking all over for you!" No, no. You make the decision—RIGHT NOW—that you are going to make a difference in your life.

So, what I'm saying is to Take. Ownership. Of. Your. Future. Success is not handed to you; it is earned. And it is *your* responsibility to earn it.

When I was about eleven, my pops sat me down, and we had a candid conversation. He explained to me the details on his successes and failures in his life. As long as I've known him, my pops has always been old. He was 43 when I was born, and he was always much older than the parents of my friends. This didn't stop him from taking it to me on the basketball court or making me run for pop flies on the baseball diamond, though. He was still energetic and active, so the advantage then, with his older age, has always been his wisdom. He had experiences that none of my other friends' parents had had, and he shared those experiences with me growing up.

This talk, though, in the kitchen, was pretty much one of those life-changing, sit-down talks. The birds and the bees conversation without talking about the birds and the bees. A serious talk that wasn't awkward.

More than anything, he explained the simplicity of work ethic. "It's one those things that you have absolute, 100%, complete control over," he told me. He explained that some things we don't have much control over at all, and we just have to take them as they come. You can't change the weather or the fact that a tree just fell on your house, and you shouldn't bother changing someone else's pessimistic attitude or your teacher's mind about the grade she gave you on your English paper. You're more or less fighting a losing battle, and your energy is best exerted elsewhere.

A lot of other things, though, we have majority, or even full, control over: our attitude; our demeanor; our willingness to accept change and deal with failure; how tough and courageous we are; or who we choose as our friends, for example.

And our work ethic. Our work ethic is one of these things that is 100%, cut and dried, within our grasp. You have the decision in the morning to get up and attack your day. Or not. That's your choice. How hard you work is a decision.

Now, I know you've heard the old cliché: work smart, not hard. "I work smart. I don't need to work hard." Right, well, of course working smart is a great idea. You should always be looking for ways to do things most efficiently with the least amount of effort. Don't cut corners, but always look for a strategic advantage.

For example, if it will take you 112 hours to learn how to build a website, you might be better off paying someone else to do it rather than trying to learn it yourself. This is working smart. Rather than busting your hump to learn about building websites, you can focus your energy on more worthy pursuits.

But! That doesn't affect your ability—and willingness—to work *hard*. Working smart just means that you can work hard elsewhere. This is a dynamic duo: working hard and working smart. Most people choose one or the other: they try to cut corners by working smart *or* they just try to put 100% of all of their effort into something without thinking about how it can be done more efficiently. Each, of course, is admirable, but you can see the value in doing both *together*, right? If you're working hard *and* smart, you're going to be a machine. You're going to take over the world. This is how you will be able to maximize whatever you are pursuing. On one hand you have your dream, your destination; on the other hand you have the steps needed to get there. The clasping of the hands, then—what makes the steps connect with the dream—comes from your willingness to dig down and get a little dirty.

The two tools here are being able to work both hard and smart. You work hard by finding any and every opportunity you can to do, say, photography. You want to get your name out there as much as possible. And when someone hires you, you go above and beyond what they ask you to do. They say take 50 pictures, you take 60. They say they want you to hang around until 10:00, you hang around until 11:00. Without being creepy. They want their photos on a disc by Wednesday, and you hire someone for $50 who can save you two hours in processing time, so that you can hand deliver those photos on a disc by Tuesday. Work hard; work smart.

You are good at what you're doing. You're doing well in school. You're doing well on the court or field or in whatever club you've joined. You're doing well at work. Et cetera. Everyone around you is proud of you.

But do you understand the difference between good and great? While you're reading these various chapters, are you starting to have perspective on where you are now and where you could be? You're doing well, let's not discount what you're already accomplishing, but there is *more* out there. There is the next level. And that's where you're heading now.

And your work ethic will get you there. When your teacher tells you to write a three-page paper, you know you can kick out three pages in an hour, no sweat. But what if you kicked that paper out in an hour, and then came back around to it, to make it even better, for another thirty minutes or so? *That* is the difference between where you are now and the next level. What you're doing will get you by, get you into college, and get you a good job. But what if you did more than just "get by." What if you did the work necessary to get into a *great* college, to get a *great* job? What if you went the extra mile? While your peers are just kicking out average work, you can kick out above average work.

And it's the same in sports or the arts or at the law firm where you work or whatever you're into. What if you lifted weights for thirty minutes after practice? What if you took some extra pitches, ran an extra mile, did a few extra sprints, took a few more shots, or watched a little bit more game film? What if you gained a second accreditation for your profession, without your boss asking you to do it?

What if you auditioned for one more part, or took an extra hour to practice your British accent? What if you stayed after band practice to practice the violin or the piano or the trumpet or the guitar for just a little while longer?

What if you did just a little bit more? You don't want to be asking these questions later in your life. Leave it all out there *now*. "What if..." is a dangerous place to be when you're older. Answer those questions *now*.

Examples of hard work abound, everywhere around you. Farmworkers are up at the crack of dawn and still out working on the fields after the sun has set. Factory workers pull twelve hour shifts, and they are often doing monotonous work. Landscapers generally get paid by the amount of work they complete, so if they hustle, they get paid well; if they slack, they'll be eating peanut butter and jelly forever.

Of course, the same dynamic exists in white-collar workers. Young attorneys pulling seventy-hour weeks so they can look good in the eyes of the partners of the firm. Med students, while doing their residencies, work ungodly hours for little pay. Financial analysts and chemical engineers and managers of textile factories and real estate agents, rocking a shirt and tie and working, in most cases, just as hard as that farmworker or that factory worker or that landscaper.

Some love it, some don't. Some farmers love what they're doing, and others don't. Some people are sitting at a desk analyzing numbers, loving life, while others dread it.

Look at Warren Buffett. Here's a dude who has spent so many days crunching numbers and analyzing businesses. If I did what he did, I'd be bored out of my flippin' mind. I don't like looking at papers and numbers and figuring out the value of things. It's hard for me. It's boring. It doesn't interest me. It would drive me mad if I had to do that for a living. But Buffett always loved it. And he never slowed down. He spent his twenties working hard, and his thirties working hard, and his forties working hard, and his fifties working hard, and his sixties, and seventies...you get the idea. He worked hard all his life. He was always looking for his advantage, a way to distinguish himself from the rest of the pack. And *hard work* was that distinction.

Warren Buffett is among the best in the world at what he has done in his life. And he got to that point for a reason.

The great ones work hard, and if you want to be great, you can and should make this same commitment.

Now, the thing is...working hard is *easy*, if you find a passion. Simple. If you love what you're doing, it is not difficult at all to work hard. You can easily be inspired and challenged to do more, do better, and get it all done quicker. When you love what you're doing, it's easy to spring out of bed in the morning and start your day with a jump, rather than dragging out of bed and needing a hit of caffeine to get you going.

It is much more difficult to work hard if you're doing things you don't want to do. I mean, think about that, right? If you have to fight through a project or a chore, it's not easy to get excited about putting in maximum effort. But if it's a hobby or a little side entrepreneurial endeavor or a sport that you love, it's easy to get out there and put in the hours required to succeed. So, I think the trick with working hard, as with many other things in life, is to ride momentum. You're going to love certain things and not love others. Even within what you love, you're going to have to do things you don't want to do. Be. Motivated. By. The. End. Goal. And find a way to enjoy the journey at the same time. Maybe you get where you'd like to go, and maybe you don't, but if you keep your eye on the prize, it will be easy to maintain a high level of effort. And as you enjoy little victories—an "A" on an exam, an incredible performance in the school play, a promotion at work—you will be inspired to keep going. Even among dealing with rejection and failure and bad times, if you are working hard you *will* enjoy little successes, and you will grow to understand the fruits and rewards that working hard brings.

And, the theory is, you will be rewarded for your hard work. Buffett's hard work made him a billionaire. Of course, everyone can't become a billionaire. It's not realistic. Actually, everyone who works hard might not even become a millionaire. It's just how it is. But this is not as much about the end result as it is the journey. You always have your goals and keep your eye on the prize, as we'll talk about, but you're also enjoying the journey. Take a moment to look back at what you did to reach your accomplishments. Take a moment to look back at the work you are currently putting in.

Maybe you love school and maybe you don't. Maybe you love your job, and maybe you don't. But don't focus on what you don't love. Focus on what you do love. Find a passion, find a purpose, and it will be relatively easy for you to work hard on the things you don't want to do, so you can do the things you do want to do.

Maybe you reach the level of Warren Buffett or whoever your hero happens to be, or maybe you don't. Time will tell. The difference you can make *right now* is your desire and determination to work hard, and appreciating the journey along the way.

The question, then, is "Why is hard work the defining characteristic among success?" Because it's the great equalizer. It's one of the only things at which everybody has an equal shot. You're born with a certain amount of talent and height and athleticism and intelligence. Of course we're not all on equal footing from birth. But from there, we get to choose whether to buck up and get after it. Or not.

Hard work separates the men from the boys, the women from the girls. If something comes easy, it comes unappreciated, right? If you don't have to work for something, you probably won't work for it. Most likely, you'll just give half effort. So, this is the way to separate those who *really* want something, from those who just *kind of* want something, those who are all talk and no walk.

Okay, so, two closing thoughts:

One, your work ethic is about managing your time well. Balance work and play. When it's time to be serious, be serious. Grind it out. And then reward yourself for the work you're doing.

Two, developing a strong work ethic is also about having pride in your work. You want to look back, and say, "Yeah, I did that." Lay it all out on the line, and see what happens. You might win; you might not. You might succeed; you might fall on your face. Who knows? But have pride in the effort you put forward. Don't look back wondering *What if?* Have pride in your work. You're creating your legacy RIGHT NOW.

Workbook 8: Managing Your Work Ethic

Key points from this session:

- William B. Sprague said, ""Do not wait till the iron is hot to strike; but make it hot by striking."
    - Don't sit around and think that opportunities will come to you.
    - You have to go out and *make* opportunities happen.
- Our work ethic is something that we have 100% control over. We can't control the weather or the tree that just fell on our house or the grade that our teacher gave us last semester. But we *can* control how hard we work.
- It is important to find the balance between working *hard* and working *smart*. Both are completely necessary.
    - Manage your time so that you are maximizing efficiency.
    - Work hard where your efforts are used effectively; have others work hard for you where their efforts are best utilized.
- It is *much* easier to work hard if you are loving what you're doing. So, GO FIND SOMETHING YOU LOVE TO DO!
    - You're always going to have to do things you don't want to do, but those things are easier if you are living your passion.
    - Hard work is the distinction between *good* and *great*.
- Working hard allows you to enjoy the journey. You might succeed; you might not. But if you are working hard in your pursuit, your efforts are rewarded by your experience.
    - You want to look back and say, "Yeah, I did that."
    - Don't look back wondering, "What if I just would have worked a little harder…"

Leadoff question: Developing a strong work ethic is much more difficult than it appears. Anyone can say, "I'm going to go out and work hard!" But it often takes more focus than empty words.

That said, take a moment to elaborate on the biggest lesson you were able to take away from this chapter?

And a quick follow-up: In addition to this one takeaway, what struck you as a positive change you can make immediately (as in, RIGHT NOW) to your daily work ethic? Surely, something hit you while you were listening...What was it? What is the one thing you can do RIGHT NOW to take your life to the next level?

The (real) world around you: It goes without saying that big time success stories (the people you see on TV or read about) are the result of a lot of grit and hard work. Reel back for a moment, though, to your peers around you rather than the people you see on TV. Based on work ethic alone (rather than natural talent or lucky connections), are you able to recognize the people around you who are going to be successful one day? There is probably someone around you about whom you can say, "_____ is going to be successful one day, because he/she works hard."

Discuss the character traits you see in them that you'd like to imitate.

Making a sacrifice: Working hard isn't always fun. Elaborate on one sacrifice you're going to have to make (something that won't necessarily be comfortable) as you move forward with a brand new work ethic. (Consider sacrifices of time or energy expended, for example.)

Quick work; quick rewards: Success is a matter of developing a work ethic that is habitual and consistent rather than spotty. That is to say, you can't work hard *some*times. You have to work hard *all* the time (while balancing your hard work with fun times, of course).

Over the next 24-48 hours, when you have a project to complete (a chore, assignment for work, or practice for a sport), put in 100% effort, more than you ever have before. If you are ordered by your parents to clean the bathroom, make it spotless. If your boss asks you to put together a presentation, make it the best presentation you've ever created. On the practice field or court, dive after every loose ball you can find.

Comment below on how this effort makes an impact on the final result. Did the bathroom look better? Did you get a better grade? Did you perform better on the field or court as a result of your effort?

But most importantly, did you *feel* more satisfied about the effort you put in as opposed to those times that you just don't give 100%?

Emulating the big dogs: As we've talked about (and will continue to talk about extensively), your success is a matter of learning lessons from those who have come before you. They have made mistakes which you can learn to avoid and they have made great decisions which you can repeat.

Over the next week, take someone successful out to lunch (or dinner or for coffee) and ask them one specific question: "What role has your work ethic played in your success?" Surely, their success is a matter of a variety of things (luck, connections, working *smart*), but it will be interesting to hear how their thoughts on work ethic mirror the thoughts in this session.

Nine

Setting Goals and Taking Action

Setting Goals and Taking Action. I've put these two concepts together for the simple reason that one can't serve without the other. After all, anybody can set goals. You can write them down, tattoo them on your arm, and scream them out at the top of your lungs. And sure, there is power in seeing your goals written down in front of you, of them materializing rather than just being thoughts. But really, it won't matter one bit without an action plan. You can really, really, really want to do something with your life—with *all* of your might—and you can really, really, really believe that it's going to happen, but if you don't take action, you're dead in the water.

The same is true for on the other side. In the last chapter, we spoke about working hard, but what good is it to just run around working hard, taking action, if you don't know what you're working for? What good is it to pursue something and you don't know what you're pursuing. Without goals, what are you shooting for? What's the point of taking action? You can work hard all day, put in long hours, but if you're doing the wrong things—if you don't know what you represent or what you're trying to accomplish—you're going to waste a lot of time, and you're going to get nowhere.

So, these two belong together. We are going to talk about the steps you need to take to set goals—the right goals—and how to take action on those goals. We're going to take a look at your life, personally, and decide what it is that you need to be doing to get to the next level. We're going to establish techniques for setting goals, to the point that by the end you'll be setting goals—short term, long term, and in the middle—without thinking about it. You're going to be so juiced up on actually taking action, that the goals you set are going to be second nature. Bing, bam, boom. Goal set, action taken, completed. Next! You're gonna be a machine.

Because listen, without a set of goals, you're just sitting on the sidelines. And without action, your goals are just words on paper.

All right, so the most important aspect to consider—and I fully intend to repeat this a couple of times over the course of this chapter—the most important aspect to consider is to set small, attainable goals first. You don't want to go in with the big one and soon find that you fall on your backside. Start small. This is okay. This is a good strategy. This is not being weak, and this is not setting yourself up for mediocrity.

Setting smaller goals does two things for you. One, it will build your confidence, but not in a superficial kind of way. You shouldn't just set goals for the sake of achieving them. "Oh, look what I achieved! I'm so great!" Achieving smaller goals sets your confidence up to handle the next level of goals. Even if you are completely and utterly failing at achieving your goals, you are in a position where you can learn from what you're doing, and that ammo allows you power to still have confidence in the next set of goals. Maybe you succeed; maybe you fail; but confidence will allow you to move forward. But! Don't. Set. Goals. Just. For. The. Sake. Of. Achieving. Them. That is lazy and weak.

More importantly, my second point, setting smaller, shorter-term goals allows you perspective on your larger goals. Is it really realistic for you to set a goal of going to medical school when you haven't even begun to test your talent or proficiency in the sciences? First, set a goal of getting a certain GPA or earning certain grades in your science classes, and then see if Med School is A) something you might be good at, and B) something you think you might be passionate about.

Set small goals first. This is *very* important for you to understand. Bigger goals can be overwhelming if you're not prepared to handle them, and you want to avoid burnout. I mean, think about it, if you set two big goals without first having a few smaller goals, you're going to lose confidence *and* you're not going to have the luxury of learning from the successes and failures of your smaller goals, right? And just the same, you want to know *specifically* what you're after. "Uh, I want to be rich and I want to graduate with honors and I want to be the CEO." Okay, many people want that. So, what do you have to do specifically to get there? What does that process look like? What are those steps? What is quantifiable? What is measurable? "I want to be rich" is a worthy goal, but it's not actionable. "I want to make $600 a week and I want to put $100 a week into a growth fund" is an actionable, measurable goal. Meet that, and then raise it to $700 if you think that's a sensible goal.

Now, none of this is to discount setting major goals. I don't want you to get the wrong impression here, and run off thinking that you should be thinking small. Indeed, this is how you start, but then it's time to extend to bigger and better things. Begin small, and then extend. Widen your scope.

Mediocre people set small goals and continue to set small goals. High achievers set small goals, and then continue to build a little bit at a time. High achievers know that there is no instant gratification, that there is no shortcut to the top, that work is required, and sometimes that work starts with baby steps. But a high achiever like you *knows* that those baby steps are simply a means to an end. A high achiever knows that nothing comes easy, and that small goals come before big goals. You need to always have your eye on the big goal, the big prize, the big dream, and you will get to that big goal after starting with smaller ones. You will have your shot with the homecoming king or queen, but only after you make smaller preparations first.

Let's think in the scope of short-term and long-term goals. I'm not going to specify a time limit on what represents a short-term goal and what represents something that is more long term. Simply, short-term goals are more for immediate attention, while longer-term goals represent the bigger picture.

Let's say that your long-term goal is to build a house on the north side of town. All the cool people live on the north side of town, and that's where you want to live. Your shorter term goals, then, might involve moving into an apartment and saving money, and then buying a small townhouse and saving money, and then moving into a little bit bigger house and saving money, all while you have your eye on the big goal: to build a house. So, your shorter-term goals—to move into an apartment and then a townhouse and then a small house—might be a year or two or three or even ten years away.

But this is all perspective. What you and I need to work on is this: break down every big dream into a series of big goals and smaller goals. And then we just keep breaking down, breaking down, breaking down, until we have a good understanding of what we need to work to achieve *right now*, so that we can get where we want to be in the future.

This is about building. Goals are about building. Building, building, building. Start short, and always look long. And after you've achieved a short-term goal, make another one. It's a cycle. Make another one, and then make another one. Each goal brings with it momentum, and if you slow up, you can quickly lose focus on your bigger goals. Ride. The. Momentum. Don't rush to get to the end, but keep a pace that will keep you going.

So, I think the trick is to concurrently work on both short-term and long-term goals. You want C, and achieving A and B will help you get there. So, you always have your eye on the big prize, but you never discount the work that is required to get to that point. A and B are essential. You understand that there are steps in this process, and that those steps are *required* rather than optional.

What are the smaller goals that you can work on now in order to get to your bigger goals later? Which steps are you taking? Are the actions that you're taking now—today, tomorrow, next Tuesday—helping you to reach your shorter-term goals? Are your actions in alignment with your end goal? Are you moving forward or are you remaining stagnant? You have a dream and a great attitude, so which goals can you set to help you achieve that dream?

Think big, act small. That's what I say. I'm sure someone else said it before me, but I'm taking credit for it. Think big; act small. Put yourself mentally at your end position. Put yourself on the field or at the concert hall or in the Emergency Room as a doctor or on the date with that foxy girl or handsome young man. In your mind, put yourself where you want to be. Take time for yourself, every day—maybe five minutes, maybe more—take time every day to put yourself at your big goal. Think about what you want first—make sure you have a solid perspective on what it is that you're looking to achieve. Sure, this can change over time, but you need to have an idea what you want. After all, having a big dream, no matter how crazy or outlandish it may be, is better than having no dream at all. In fact, if you gave me two options: if you gave me the option to have a big dream and no talent—at anything—or the option to have no dream but lots of talent, I'll take no talent, any day. Any day. I'll develop the skills along the way. But if I don't have a dream, if I don't have an idea what I'm shooting for, my talent is, essentially, wasted.

If you would like to lose weight, then you can set smaller incremental goals in your pursuit of having a beach body. Don't look at it and say, "Ugh, I have to lose fifty pounds?" That's too much. It appears insurmountable. Fifty pounds might as well be five hundred. Say, "Okay, I'm going to lose four pounds per month." Then, in a year, after twelve months of losing four pounds at a time, you are right there at your goal weight. Fifty pounds appears unreachable. Four pounds at a time is very reachable.

And so the next step here, then, is to take action. Talk is cheap. Setting goals is easy. Action is hard.

So, I'll call back briefly to several of the things we've already spoken about in earlier chapters.

First, manage your work ethic. Understand when you're setting your goals that there is a balance between challenge and attainability. You want to set a goal that is going to be a challenge for you to accomplish—you want to make yourself put in the work—however you don't want to set something that is so tough that, by extension, it is also unattainable. "I'm going to make a million dollars by next Thursday! Let's go get 'em!" Set your goals in such a way that you know you are going to have to put in work, but you know that the work you put in can be rewarded.

The second thing, then, is to make sure you are able to maintain a high level of enthusiasm, for everything from your small goals to your big dream. Be passionate. Like we talked about, if you're not passionate—if you lose your enthusiasm—then what's the point? Your goals are going to be challenging and tough, sure, but if you're not having fun along the way, then you need to get out. You're going to be pressed—running three miles in the morning is not necessarily fun, nor is eating broccoli when you've gotten used to eating burgers and fries—but those sacrifices come with rewards, and those rewards are more fun than any kind of instant gratification you can obtain from a greasy burger or salty fries. You don't have to agree with me right now. You'll see. Be passionate about losing weight, and make the sacrifices, and you'll see the rewards. Be passionate about what you can accomplish on the field or the stage or the classroom, and you'll see the rewards.

Set goals—large and small—and be passionate about those goals.

Action. That's what we're talking about here. You are going to follow through. You are ACTION-oriented. Not only do you intend to wake up in the morning, attack your day, and succeed, you are actually going to do it. I'm telling you that this is what can be different about your life, starting today. Set a goal, and work to reach it.

For example, if someone is thirsty, they can say, "Golly, I'm thirsty," or they can get up and go about finding something to drink. They can hope *all day long* that they will find a bottle of water, but if they don't actually take action, they will remain thirsty.

Stop hoping, and start making moves. It doesn't matter if you want something. It matters that you get up and get after it, go about finding what you want.

By the way, tracking back to the idea of strategies for setting goals: Be. Specific. About. Your. Goals. This is another great technique. Rather than setting twelve goals that are all over the place, set three or four that are specific to what you're trying to accomplish. I have some great friends—good people with great ideas and a lot of ambition—who lose out on a lot of opportunity, because their lives are spread too thin. They're going in too many different places. Reel it in. What do you love? What are you passionate about? What, specifically, do you want? The old adage, "You can't have it all," is not only true, for the most part, but these are words that you should live by. You should go in with the understanding that you can't have *everything*. You can have a lot, and you can achieve great things, but you shouldn't say, "I wanna do this and this and this and this and this and, oh yeah...definitely that." It's a losing proposition. Narrow your focus to two or three things. Set two or three goals and focus on those goals with everything you have. Five or ten or fifteen goals can have you spread all over the place and leave you broken down and burned out. Be GREAT at something; not GOOD at a bunch of things. Did you hear that? Be GREAT at something; not GOOD at a bunch of things.

Now, are your goals going to develop over time? Of course. You say, "My goal is to secure five new clients before the end of the year," and you get out there and discover that it's more important for you to secure three new clients and spend the rest of your time fostering your relationships with those three. No problem. Revisit and revise your goals, but don't just bail on them because they're hard. Don't make excuses to cover missed goals. Be honest with yourself. Adjust your goals to the lifestyle you'd like to lead, and remember that the higher the goal, the higher the reward. Looking back, you're always moving forward. Learn from your mistakes, and adjust your outlook, and *always* keep your eyes straight ahead.

So, the final step, then, as we've already talked about in earlier sessions is to evaluate your progress, to go back and learn from your failures and successes. Be careful here, though. You don't want to get too caught up in the outcome. Setting goals and taking action is the hard part, sure, but you have 100% control over those two entities. The outcome? Not so much. There are other various things that can come into play. Not excuses, but just extraneous factors. If you set a goal to run a marathon in six months, and you break your ankle, are you going to hate yourself for not succeeding? No. You set your goals, you woke up every day at 6 to train, and you hit a roadblock. You can't be mad about that. Be mad if you aren't setting goals and taking action in the first place. Remove yourself from the outcome: learn from it, appreciate it, but focus on the journey, and the journey, in this case, is your ability to figure out what it is what you want, write it down, and go get after it.

Set goals, take action, and ask questions later.

Workbook 9: Setting Goals and Taking Action

Key points from this session:

- *Anybody* can set goals. *Anybody* can say, "I want to _____."
  - But few people *act* on those goals.
  - It takes a special person to follow through with the goals he or she has set.
- Without setting goals, you're just sitting on the sideline. And without taking action, your goals are just words on paper.
- Set small, attainable goals first. And then build from there.
  - In school, you set the small goal of getting an "A" on a test in order to achieve your larger goal of getting an "A" in the class.
  - In business, you test market a product before you roll out with it.
  - In your social life, you get various things in order FIRST before you reach for your bigger, longer-term goal of dating the homecoming king or queen.
- Think of your big dream and then think about the smaller goals you can set in order to achieve that bigger dream.
  - Before they get on the radio, musicians have to: start a band; practice; play smaller venues; play at a music festival; save money to cut an album; mail that album out; play on college radio; etc.
  - Before they play in front of a huge crowd, professional softball players have to: build leg strength; make the high school team; work on hitting and pitching; play college ball; work on running speed and fielding; etc.
- The biggest step, then, is to take action.
  - Talk is cheap.
  - Take action.
- The final step is to evaluate your progress and your successes and failures as they relate to your future course of setting goals and taking action.

Leadoff question: Regarding setting goals, perhaps you have reached a different level of understanding after reading this chapter: everybody knows how to set goals (anyone can paste their goals next to their bed), but you are starting to see the value in actually *taking action* on those goals.

Discuss below how your views on setting and taking action on goals (in a broad sense) have *changed* after listening to chapter 9. How do you feel now as opposed to how you felt last week?

Name one thing you specifically took away from this session.

Calling back to failure: Reaching one of your goals (large or small) is very satisfying. It can be equally heartbreaking, though, to set a goal and *not* reach that goal.

Talk about one goal that you have set and failed to achieve. Large or small, how did it feel for you to fall short of something that you worked to achieve? What could you have done differently (or what *did* you do differently) to achieve your goal next time?

Most importantly, did you grow from the experience of falling short?

9. Setting Goals and Taking Action

Your goals, now! Think about one big goal, one big dream of yours. Below, list 5 smaller goals that you can achieve en route to achieving that one big goal or dream.

1.

2.

3.

4.

5.

Taking action, now! Now that you understand that listing your goals is most effective when you establish a means of action, list 5 things you can do (one by one) to take action to achieve these goals.

1.

2.

3.

4.

5.

Now, take this sheet of paper and put it somewhere that you'll see it every day (by your bed, in the bathroom, in your backpack). Live by these goals and live by the course of action you can take to achieve these goals.

Exchanging ideas: You're not the only one who sets goals. Everybody does, whether they write them down or not.

Now is a great time to be accountable for your goals. Call one of your friends, a friend who is an achiever and a goal setter, someone who knows what they want. This can be a teammate, a neighbor, a possible business partner, or a classmate. Share your goals with them, and then exchange ideas on what you each can do to achieve these goals.

Tomorrow morning: Now that you understand the value in taking action as part of the process of achieving your goals, list two things you are going to do immediately—starting tomorrow morning—to achieve one of the goals on your list. Don't wait two or three days or until next weekend. What are you going to do NOW?

Furthermore, reflect on what those two actions can specifically mean for your long term success.

Ten

Embracing Change

I don't know you, but I do know that you are starting to see a change here, even already. A dramatic change? Nah. But subtle ones. I wouldn't expect a dramatic change until later down the line. You are going to build your life from these sessions rather than expect some miraculous achievement to occur. There is no quick fix, but there are opportunities to lay a firm foundation for a bright future. And that's what you're doing.

So, I'd imagine that you are starting to see small, slight changes, and this is great. This is how it should be. When you set out to make a big move in your life, you are inspired by the little moves. They keep you going. If I want to lose fifty pounds, once I see that I've lost five pounds, I see a small change—in the mirror and the way that I feel—and that encourages me to keep going. "Man, I look good. I mean, really good!" So, appreciate these small changes, and use them as momentum for what's to come.

But! This is not the kind of change that we are here to talk about today. That is the good change—the "Hey, look at me, I'm a total rockstar" change. The change that you *want*, that you *embrace*, that you *welcome*.

The change we're going to talk about today is more along the lines of the "This is awkward and scary" kind of change, the kind of change that many of us do not like to confront, or, in many circumstances, even talk about. You know what I'm talking about: new school, new classes, new friends, new team, new neighborhood, new job, new boss, new tennis racket...new whatever. We're talking about the kind of change that you approach with sweaty palms and shaky, wobbly legs. Your first day of high school, your first practice on the varsity volleyball team, or having to cope with a divorce, let's say. This change isn't fun or exciting or easy to handle. This kind of change takes a special person or special circumstances...or both. This kind of change takes grit and guts and maybe a screw loose or two.

But at the same time, this kind of change is the change of champions. There isn't a single successful person who hasn't had to learn to embrace change. In fact, I'll go one step further, and say that those who *don't* embrace change are pretty much spot-on guaranteed to remain in the same mediocre life that they've thus far grown accustomed to. A life lacking change is a life lacking substance. And a life lacking substance lacks the ingredients for success. Think about that for a second: if you don't have the ingredients to make a pizza, then you aren't going to be able to make a pizza. You need flour and cheese and sauce and pepperoni and onions—or whatever you like to have on your pizza. And if you don't have those ingredients, either you're not going to be able to make the pizza or the pizza won't be the same.

And when you find yourself at a higher altitude, with thinner air and a gas oven instead of the electric one that you're used to, do you abandon plans to make a pizza altogether or do you make adjustments?

It's the same with change. If you don't have the ingredients to handle change—or if you don't handle change at all—you're going to have a rough go. Success *requires* change, which leaves one of two choices for you: embrace it or run from it. And the decision you make about how you're going to adapt your life will directly correlate to the success that you will enjoy. Or not. Change is proportionate to success. This is a fact. Studies have been done—by some really smart people with big computers and pencils and lab coats and dorky glasses—studies have been done by these gurus and geniuses that show the correlation between people adapting to change and their success. Those who adapt to change, win. Those who don't adapt to change, lose.

This. Is. A. Choice. That. We. Make. We adapt well to change or we don't. Are you starting to see a trend here with a lot of the things we're talking about? That trend is one word: choice. We can't control our friends' behavior or our teachers' behavior or our boss's behavior, but we can control our behavior. We can *choose* how we deal with failure and various problems that we face and how we manage our work ethic, and now I'm telling you that we get to *choose* how we deal with change. That's what I'm telling you here.

Stepping out of your comfort zone and embracing change is a very important component to taking your life to the next level. Get out of your little bubble! Stop being so regimented and living in the little world where you do what everybody else does. Embrace. Change.

Now, think for a moment, how this applies to you, to your world. What has been a big change in your life? How did you handle it? Did you embrace it or did you run from it? I'm not judging you. Maybe you made the right decision or maybe you didn't. How did you handle your moment of change? Are you proud of what you did? Or would you do things differently next time?

Are you going through something, through a change, right now? Of course you are! Maybe it's small or maybe it's a bigger change, but we are *always* dealing with some kind of change. Remember the section on problem solving? We *always* have problems, large or small, and we're *always* having to put out little fires. Same with change: large or small, you are *always* going to have to deal with a changing world, with a changing environment around you. Especially today. Today, our world is a whirlwind. So many people are working to advance our society forward. And with technological developments, it's so easy. I have an idea today, I can have it out tomorrow, and all of a sudden, I'm sponsoring change. It's crazy.

So, as you go through these changes you're going through now—I'm talking about right now, today, tomorrow, and next Tuesday—as you're going through these changes, understand two things: One, these changes are inevitable. Deal with them, handle them with charisma, and face change head on rather than running from it.

Two, change is change, whether it is large or small. And the way that you handle change—embracing it or running from it—carries from your smaller issues to your bigger ones. If you handle smaller issues well, you will be poised to handle bigger issues. If you *can't* handle smaller issues, smaller moments of change, how can you expect to deal with bigger issues? Y'know what I mean?

So, practice how you handle change on smaller issues. Smaller change might mean your parents switching cereals, or the kind of meals your husband or wife is serving in the evening. Or where you're going on vacation. Or taking the lead on a project at work when you're used to merely being a member of the team.

These are not major issues. These are smaller issues. You can and should be able to handle them. But they are still change. You still have the opportunity to whine or to embrace these issues. "Ah, Ma. Do we *have* to eat this kind of cereal? This is ridiculous. I don't think I'll like Toasty Chocolate Puffs." Calm down. It's cereal. Deal with it. Stop whining. You've never even tried Toasty Chocolate Puffs, so how do you know if you'll like them or not?

The same goes with taking point on a project at work. It will be a challenge for you, stepping away from being a follower and into a leadership role. You will have to work longer hours. It will be stressful. People will love you, and people will hate you. But if you take it head on rather than tip-toeing in, your coworkers will see that you are serious about creating something valuable. and they will get on board with you. *That* is embracing change.

And if you can handle these smaller issues, these smaller changes, then you will be much more poised to handle bigger issues. If your parents separate or you are forced to move for work or go through a tough situation like getting into a car accident, you still get to choose how you handle this major change. Remember, you can't control it. *You* don't have the power to change it. This is your school; this is your family and professional life; the accident already happened. The question is, "What are you going to do now?" How are you going to adapt?

I've spoken with a lot of different people, from administrators to professional businesspeople at the top of their industry, and one of the biggest things they wish more of their employees would understand is how to cope with change. This is a *major* skill, and it is something that can set you apart from your peers, from your competition. I'm telling you that you want to welcome change into your life with open arms.

Think outside the box. Okay, great, so you know *how* to deal with change. That's awesome. Now, the next step, then, is to invite change. To seek it out. It's not enough to put up your defenses and be prepared for the blows that come your way. You need to go out there and strike a couple of blows yourself. Remember the earlier chapter on *Having The Courage To Be Different*? Remember how we talked about thinking outside the box. This goes hand in hand with your ability to adapt to change. Adapting to change, embracing change, often involves going out after it. And that's what I hope you're able to take away here. Don't be normal. Don't be like everybody else. While you're rolling with the times, accepting change in your life, why not go out there into the world to find change? Why not attack change? I mean, if it's coming anyway, why not meet it halfway—or more? Why wait for it?

Look for change. Invite it. And embrace it.

Change is imminent. It is *going* to happen. Don't think you can avoid it. Death, taxes, and change.

The only thing you can do is to connect your vision—where you're headed—with your willingness to change. Maybe you win; maybe you lose. Max McKeown said that "Change is inevitable; progress is not." In fact, success and change aren't even necessarily correlated. Once you get to a certain point in your life doesn't mean that you get to just lie down and cruise through on an unswerving path. Change will *always* be there. And that's why it is important to learn techniques for handling it *now*, so that it will be habitual by the time a lot more is on the line when you're older.

But this is no reason to be depressed. Like, "Oh, the evil change is coming, so you need to be ready for it. Better pack an umbrella." Not at all. Change is good. Change is fun. Change will take your life to the next level...depending upon how you handle it. I'm simply telling you that if you go out and get after it, if you take change with a smile, you will be happier, healthier, and wiser. Don't be down about change. Change is great and exciting. Change is an adventure. You don't know what's going to happen today, tomorrow, or the next day, but if you take it with the outlook that this is another great adventure in your life, the next move of your life—whatever it is—can work in your favor.

Nothing lasts forever. Nothing. Not one thing. "Well, uh, Adam, uh, I hate to break it to you, but, uh, the sky lasts forever." Okay, fine. I don't even know what that means, but whatever.

The sky lasts forever. But even that is changing on a daily basis, so certainly in 100 years, 1000 years, a million years, the universe is going to be different than it is right now. I mean, look up at the clouds next time you're outside. Do you see those clouds moving? Exactly. Changing. Rock formations change over time, mountains move over time, water levels in a lake change over time. So, whether it's your skill on the volleyball court developing on a daily basis, your lifestyle changing from year to year, or a certain type of duck that becomes extinct over the course of 5000 years—whatever the life cycle is—things are *always* changing. Nothing lasts forever.

Now, one more thing before we close up here. I'm presenting some important ideas here, and I'm certain you are taking some valuable lessons away, since these thoughts are tried and proven, and most of them have come from other people anyway, from books and articles and whatnot that I've read over the course of my life. Everything I'm reciting has come from authorities who are much more intelligent than I am.

But, you have to understand, and I'm sure you're getting this by now, that you have to think on your own, think critically. Always question, "Okay, how does this apply to *my* life? What would *I* do in that situation? Does this make sense for me?"

In most cases, it will. These are tactics that *will* take your life to the next level, techniques you *need* in order to enjoy the success you would like.

In some cases, though, you have to think for yourself. And that's precisely how it is with change. Change is imminent—GUARANTEED, going to happen—and maybe there are times when you roll with it, and maybe there are times when you say, "Naw, that's just not for me." Going to college is a good example. Some of my friends went close to home just because that was comfortable, and some went far away. I went to college thirteen hours from home, my brother went to college ninety minutes from home, and my dad went to college, literally a five minute walk from the childhood home where he grew up in Chapel Hill, North Carolina. Some people know the extent to which they can handle living outside the box. What kind of change are you preparing yourself to deal with? Start small, and develop and grow to appreciate change over time. You don't *have* to dive in head first. You'll get there. College is change enough for many people, and going far away from home might not make the most sense for you. Or maybe it does. Don't *burden* yourself with change. Don't abuse it. Appreciate it. Embrace it.

You need to be out there, and you need to live your life outside of your little box, but you also need to understand how to manage change. How can you maximize the results of change? Take it with a smile, head held high, and understand that change is good to the extent that you don't abuse it.

So, gauge change on *your* terms. Many things you have to take, sure, and you won't get a say.

But other times, you will have to ask yourself how much change you are willing to tolerate. My experience has been that those who get after it and look for moments of change—whether large or small—are better-prepared for life situations, and are therefore more successful.

Those. Who. Are. Prepared. To. Tackle. Change. Are. More. Successful. No doubt about it.

Workbook 10: Embracing Change

Key points from this session:

- One constant in life is change. Good change; bad change; all kinds of change.
    - From your social life to your academic life to your professional life.
    - And if you can effectively learn how to deal with change *now*, you will be far ahead of your peers *later*.
- *Dealing* with change is one thing, though. *Embracing* and *attacking* it (welcoming it!) is what can set you up for the next level.
    - Don't shy away from change. And don't just wait for it to come to you.
    - Go out and meet change halfway. Seek it out, even.
- Embracing change is a matter of stepping outside of your comfort zone. Sometimes you're going to have to make the sacrifice of doing things that might be a little bit cumbersome or inconvenient.
- Dealing with smaller changes is great practice for embracing bigger ones.

Leadoff question: This session is important to grasp as you begin—or continue—to think critically. What is the ONE big thing you learned from this session? What is your big takeaway? This can be a story, a lesson, a tactic, a call to action, or, well, anything.

Most importantly, how does this session apply *specifically* to you?

Analyzing others' adaptability to change: Bigwigs have many of the same issues dealing with change as you do. Remember, no matter where you are in life, change is imminent.

Think about someone famous (a musician, an athlete, an actor, a politician, etc.), and consider a change they've had to deal with (a tragedy, a career change, a sudden surge of popularity). Analyze how they handled this moment of change.

Did they do it effectively? Would you have done anything differently?

10. Embracing Change

Your adaptability to change: Think about the last major change in your life. Maybe this was a move, a change of schools, or a tragedy in your family's life.

How did you handle it? Are you happy with how you handled it? Did you make rational decisions? Could you have done a better job handling it or were you happy with your decisions? Would you have done anything differently?

Did this situation properly prepare you for the next time you will have to deal with change?

Looking forward: One of the best techniques for problem solving is your ability to solve problems *before* they happen. And the same can be said about handling change: if you are able to foresee when change is coming, you will be well-equipped to embrace it.

Below, list 5 changes (large or small) that you will potentially have to deal with in the next year. Think about your family, social, academic, and professional lives:

1.

2.

3.

4.

5.

Making the most: Now, put yourself in a position not just to *deal* with these changes but to *maximize* your opportunities.

List below the 5 ways that you can capitalize on the changes you listed above. How can you work these changes into your favor? (For example: if you listed a change of schools above, you can capitalize on that change by stepping outside of your comfort zone and committing to swap old school stories with three new peers every day during your first week of school.)

1.

2.

3.

4.

5.

Eleven

Toughness

The whining, the complaining, the calling out "Poor me". It's pervasive. It's everywhere. Now, before you get all riled up and playing the gender card, hear this: this is not a male/female thing. "Oh, but Shep, I'm just a sweet young girl. I'm sensitive. I have pigtails and bows in my hair. I'm not supposed to be tough." I hear you, but maybe we need to define what toughness is all about. Toughness is not going up to someone in the hallway and smacking them upside the head and taking their milk money. Toughness is winning, but toughness is not winning *at any cost*. Toughness is not one's ability to show that they are better or more important or more powerful than someone else. Toughness doesn't mean having an armful of tattoos and wearing tight t-shirts, and saying things like, "Hey, you mind spotting me real quick on this set. I'm 'bout to crush this workout."

Actually, in many cases, it's the opposite.

I'm talking about mental toughness. I'm talking about your ability to look past your falls, flops, humiliations, rejections, failures, setbacks, and mistakes, and move along. *That* is toughness. *That* is what you need to be focusing on. Anybody can hit the weights and eat smoothies and egg whites in the morning and become physically tough. Mental toughness is more of a challenge to develop. This kind of toughness is committing to do your best, all the time, without exception. Toughness is getting knocked down and getting back up. Toughness is hearing someone say, "You sure are one ugly son of a gun," and turning to walk away rather than firing back.

Toughness is not retaliation or showing somebody up. Toughness is recognizing, in yourself, that you *can* do better and you *will* do better. Toughness is getting back up.

Quit cryin'. Quit complainin'. As said in the classic film *Shawshank Redemption:* "Get busy living or get busy dying."

I've had a lot of experience with toughness. Physically, I'm really not a tough guy. I'm 6'2" and relatively lean, and I have a very soft exterior. I'm sensitive. I like to cuddle more than anything. True, when it comes to board games, I am tough and ruthless, but even then, I don't want to be malicious and try to purposefully hurt anyone or get under their skin. I'm just a pleasant dude who won't stop until I have the trophy in my hand. And if you get in my way, I'll ask you nicely to move.

Maybe you can relate to what I'm saying or maybe not. Maybe you have a pressing issue in your life. Maybe you are facing illness or you've been in a serious accident or had to deal with a major loss. I'm not telling you to just dismiss any of these issues. Embrace them. Cry about them. Whether someone is picking on you or someone close to you has passed away and you miss them miserably; whether it is what you consider a minor issue or a major issue is unimportant. I'm not telling you to just "toughen up" and grow up and forget about it and act like it didn't happen.

I'm simply saying that there are mature ways to deal with the issue. Once you've had the opportunity to vent your frustrations or sadness about something, the next step is to go about resolving your issue, to invoke the tactics on problem solving that we've already talked about. *That* is toughness.

My friend Hal Elrod has three words that get him to work his way through the tough times. "Can't change it." Bam. That's it. Can't change it. Whenever you're in a tight spot, there is one of two things that you can do: change it. Or not. If you do have the power to change it, go about making that happen. Otherwise, make the determination that you can't do anything about it, and it's best to work *with* it than *against* it.

You got into a car accident. Can't change it.

You got fired. Can't change it.

Your team lost. Can't change it.

Your mom has cancer. Can't change it.

This isn't ruthless or insensitive. Do you avoid or sidestep these problems? No, of course not. When you lose a game, you get mad, you get angry, and you figure out what you did wrong. Double down on your practice sessions. When someone close to you is stricken with a disease, you grieve. But if you harp on these issues, this will get you *nowhere*. Nowhere. I'm telling you. Nowhere. Cry, complain, and vent your frustrations for about three minutes, and then toughen up. Take action. It's cool to be sad and angry and mad, but it's not cool for these feelings to persist without making moves. When someone in your life gets cancer or passes away, this is a *horrible* moment. Both of my parents have gone through cancer; it is a wicked disease. But if you can't change it, the question is then, "All right, what are we going to do now?"

This is toughness.

Toughness, by the way, is toning down your ego just a little bit. Okay, maybe a lot. We'll talk about this more in the final chapter, but *you have got to let go of your ego*. Seriously. Leggo your ego. In America, we are, for whatever reason, a strangely arrogant nation. I don't understand why. I'm not picking on *you*. I'm picking on *all* of us. As it relates to toughness, we just think everything is going to be all right, and then, when it isn't, we point fingers and blame and play the victim.

That isn't toughness. Toughness is accountability. Toughness is saying, "Dangit, I messed that up, and dangit, I'm going to fix it." That's tough. For some reason, we don't do that. We lay blame elsewhere. We're soft. We're weak. We aren't mature. We aren't strong.

You can change this trend in your life. *You* can make a difference. Let everybody else be weak. Let them struggle. Let them blame and be generally unaccountable. You want the edge? I'm giving you the edge right here, right now. You want to be the greatest, you want to be successful, you want to take your life to the next level, and I'm telling you right now how you can do that: be tougher. Be accountable. Stand up for what is right in your life, and stand against what isn't right. Dig in a little deeper. Challenge someone, but don't be a jerk about it. Just stand up a little. Stand up for what you represent. If you see someone littering or you hear someone using a racially slanderous word, call them on it. Don't be malicious or cruel, but let them know, "Hey, that ain't cool."

See, here's the thing. Don't tell me you had a bad day. We all have bad days. When you sit down to dinner tonight, no matter what it is—Kentucky Fried Chicken, pizza, or a hearty home-cooked meal—whatever you're eating tonight, you just remember that somebody else out there has it worse than you have it. That's a fact. And if you can maintain perspective on that, you're ahead of the game. In college, a friend of mine used to complain *all the time* about the food served in the cafeteria. Another friend of mine recently got a vacation from her parents—to Colorado— and she whined, because she wanted to go to the Bahamas. "I don't want to go skiing. I want to go on a cruise."

Boo flippin' hoo.

That's not tough. That's weak. Just think, there is someone out there who is legitimately struggling, who has real problems. And we're complaining about the temperature of our hotel room and that the soup our waiter just served us isn't the optimal temperature. Get serious. Every minute you spend being weak and soft and worrying about problems that you have no control over, every minute you spend exerting negative energy like that is a minute you aren't able to exert positive energy, time you could be spending moving forward. Think of *that* scale. Negative energy is not just negative energy; it's negative energy plus it's not positive energy.

If you're moving backward, you're moving in the wrong direction *and* you're not moving in the right direction. Not only are you going *nowhere*, you're going to a bad place.

I'll tell you about toughness. I just thought of a great example. You ever heard of John Foppe?

Yes? No? Doesn't matter. You can Google him later, but I'm going to tell you about him right now, anyway. This dude was born with no arms. No arms. Like, I mean, do you understand what that means? No arms. Look at your arms, and think about everything you do with your arms. I do everything with my arms. I even talk with my arms. But John doesn't have any arms. So when he was a toddler, he began to train himself to eat with his feet...he learned how to bring a spoon to his mouth with his feet. I have trouble getting into a comfortable situation to sit with my legs crossed, and this dude is learning how to eat with his feet. That's crazy to me.

Today, John drives, skies, writes, and paints with his legs, feet, and toes. Drives, skies, writes, and paints. I mean, COME ON! This dude doesn't have any arms.

That, ladies and gentlemen, is toughness. He saw a situation, a problem, and rather than say, "Hmmmmm...this just really sucks. I think I'm going to go sit in the corner for the rest of my life and complain," he immediately started training himself to live life to the fullest. That's a tough dude.

So, whatever your situation is, whatever your limitation is, think about how you can overcome it. Life is tough! Life is not easy. But it's not supposed to be. It's supposed to be a challenge. You're not supposed to be able to just wake up in the morning, and BAM! a light turns on and everything is just peachy. You're supposed to work for it. Otherwise, how can you possibly appreciate it, right?

This is what toughness is all about. Nothing has ever come easy for John Foppe. But he doesn't wake up in the morning and question his life or think about how someone else has it better than he does. "Why me? What did I do wrong to deserve this?" No. He wakes up, says that today is going to be a great day, me and my body without arms, and he goes about living his life to the fullest. He's done more in his life than most people who have arms, and that's pretty amazing.

I'm just saying that if he can do what he has done, if he can accomplish what he has been able to accomplish, what is our excuse? What is my excuse? What is your excuse?

That should be your mantra: "What is my excuse?" And the answer should always be: "I don't make excuses."

Toughness is going to extend from now and for the rest of your life: in your academic life, in your social life, in your athletic life, in your professional life, and in your family life as a parent or a spouse.

Representing toughness now will allow you to be prepared for the much larger issues in your life that come later. Toughness is really represented when pressure strikes. I mean think about it: it's easy to be tough when life is good. You don't have any real adversity to face when life is good. Toughness is a commodity rather than a necessity. But then, when a challenging moment strikes, toughness will prevail. That's what separates the men from the boys and the women from the girls.

And I'm telling you that you can prepare yourself *now* for those tough times later.

Moreover, your toughness will be a reflection of how others perceive you. If you are perceived as weak, people will walk over you—now and forever. If you let people walk all over you, *you will not win.* But if you buck up, and take charge, and stand your ground, you will have a reputation as someone who isn't soft or weak, rather strong and tough. People will take you more seriously. They'll want to work with you on various projects and they'll want to just generally associate themselves with you. A tough persona represents success. Be tough; be successful. This is the perception—the aura—that you want to give off.

Listen: It is inevitable that you are going to face challenging situations in your life, times when your toughness will have to prevail. It's going to happen. People get ill, accidents happen; you're going to be an athlete on the sidelines; you're going to have to take a job you don't want to take in order to work your way through school or because, well, you just can't find another job. It will happen. Sorry. Deal with it. This is life. Life is tough.

Just the same, life is also very rewarding. Tough situations allow you to appreciate the end result of working through them. You wait tables for four years, and that college degree is going to feel pretty sweet, a little bit sweeter because of what you went through to earn it. You fight through an injury, and you're going to really appreciate your time on the field when you're healthy. You understand what I'm talking about here? Toughness. Prevails. In. The. End.

So, here we are. Whatever definition toughness represents for you, moving forward, I'll let you have it, but the point is that a real tough guy or gal is marked by the way that he treats others.

Walking away from a fight? That's tough.

Staying up late to put extra effort into a paper rather than settling for the mediocre one you've already written? That's tough.

Shaking hands with the enemy? That's tough.

Reworking a powerpoint presentation that wasn't *precisely* what your boss wanted—and doing it without complaining? That's tough.

Cooking dinner for your husband or wife after a long, hard day? That's tough. I'm not talking about a Valentine's Day dinner; I'm talking about on a Tuesday, a random day when it isn't expected.

Toughness prevails every time.

Workbook 11: Toughness

Key points from this session:

- Toughness is not designated to one gender or another.
  - Males can be tough.
  - Females can be tough.
- We're talking about mental toughness here. After all, *anybody* can be physically tough, but it takes a truly strong person to be mentally tough.
  - This doesn't mean having a rough persona or acting like you're better than everyone else.
  - Toughness is not retaliation or showing somebody up.
  - You can cry and be sensitive once in a while and still be tough. There is a balance between toughness and sensitivity. Toughness is dealing with the various issues in your life and then moving on.
- Determine if you can change the situation you're in. If you can, great. If you can't change it, though, focus your efforts elsewhere.
  - We ALL have bad days. What can YOU do to handle your bad day?
- Toughness is toning down your ego just a little bit.
- If you can establish mental toughness NOW, you will be far ahead of your peers LATER. Your toughness will come out when you are facing a stressful situation.
  - It's easy to be tough when life is good.
  - But when you face true adversity—now or in the future—your true toughness will come out.

11. Toughness

Leadoff question: After reading this chapter, take a moment to rate your own toughness. Do you think you're tough? When something bad happens, are you well equipped, mentally, to handle it? And when something good happens, do you immediately act to capitalize on it?

Your toughness, now: Each person who reads this chapter on toughness tends to take something different away. Considering your one or two major takeaways from this session, what is one positive change you can make *immediately* (as in, RIGHT NOW) to the way you handle the troubling situations that come your way.

What is ONE major improvement you can make to your level of mental toughness?

The (real) world around you: There's no question that most successful people are tough. Regardless of the persona they assume in the media, they have had to face all kinds of adversity and scrutiny during their rise to the top.

Open up the closest magazine or turn on the TV to a news program, and select the first famous person that you come across (whether you like him or her or not). In the space below, discuss how you think that person's mental toughness played a role in his or her rise to the top.

Toughness as a sacrifice: For the most part, being tough is a matter of making sacrifices. It isn't easy to dig deep to work yourself out of a sad situation; it isn't easy to suck it up and shake hands with someone you don't like; it isn't easy to bounce back after a major loss.

But it must be done.

What is one major event where you reacted well, with toughness? How did you handle that situation better than any other that you've ever had to handle?

11. Toughness

Showing weakness: Conversely, you can surely recollect a time where you didn't handle a challenging situation very well.

Without looking back with regret, you can always learn from these mistakes. What would you have done differently? Is it possible that a little bit stronger mental toughness could have played a role in handling the situation better? How so?

Acting on your newfound mental toughness: Developing a permanent state of mental toughness takes practice. It starts with how you handle your next challenging situation, and builds from there.

Small or large, within the next 24 hours you will face a difficult situation. Maybe this will be an internal struggle or perhaps it will be a problem you have with someone else at school, at work, or on the playing field.

In three or four sentences, discuss how you handled this situation with toughness:

Twelve

Supreme Preparation

I want you to think about a recent event you participated in—a game, a meeting, a test, an interview. Something within the last week where you were a little nervous/anxious/excited about the outcome. Something where you were invested in the end result, and you fought hard for a successful one.

Now, I want you to think about the preparation you did for that event. From the beginning of time until the moment you stepped into the classroom or on the playing field, for example. Think about both the physical preparation and the mental preparation that you put into performing this task.

My question for you, then, is this: Do you think you were fully prepared? Whether you won or not, whether you got an A on the test or a C, do you think you were fully prepared? Forget success or failure for a moment. Sometimes you succeed when ill-prepared, and sometimes you fail when well-prepared. But with this *one* event that you are thinking about, do you feel you were fully prepared? Could you have done better? Could you have put yourself in a better position to succeed? Could you have, in fact, performed better if you would have been better prepared?

Today, we are here to talk about just that: Supreme Preparation. A *lot* of tools are needed for preparation, and you have to have many things in order before you can begin the process of preparation. The tools you accumulate, the tools we've been working to accumulate here—accountability, dealing with change, rejection, and failure, your work ethic, organization, problem solving, etcetera, etcetera—all of these tools are what get you prepared, right? Prepared for the good times and bad. Prepared for things you can expect—like that test or a job interview or a presentation to a major client, for example—and prepared for the things you might not expect—

an injury, an accident, or abruptly getting laid off from your job, for example.

Supreme preparation covers all fronts, expected and unexpected. Preparation isn't necessarily just knowing what to do in a certain situation; preparation is knowing how to make the most of it. You don't want to be mediocre, average. You don't want to be neutral. C'mon. Seriously. Who wants *that*? You want to be able to take a situation, whatever it is, and you want to be prepared to benefit from on it, profit from it, get the most out of it, and *maximize* every bit of that situation that you can.

I'm telling you that you can be ahead of the game. I mean, think about it, if you are prepared for all of these issues—good or bad—*before* they happen, don't you think you're going to be better off. If you are able to troubleshoot problems before they happen, don't you think you'll be better equipped to handle them? If you're prepared for successful moments before they happen, don't you think you'll be better prepared to capitalize on them? Seriously. Think about that. Think about the power in your ability to deal with a situation instantaneously because you are better suited to deal with it.

So, from the standpoint that you already are developing the tools to be prepared, you are far ahead of the game. You've been working your way through these sessions and filling out the workbooks with such ferocity that you have an acute perspective on what it takes to deal with change and work hard and effectively solve problems and, in general, take your life to the next level.

Now, what we need to do is work on taking the tools you've acquired, the lessons you've learned and bottling them up into the most efficient system of preparation possible. Because, really, preparation is the difference between average and great, right? You don't make a fantastic soufflé or quiche or chicken dinner—or whatever it is that you make when it's your turn to cook—without preparing the food first. You don't just take a chicken, stick it in the oven, wait an hour, pull it out, and dig in. Of course not. You're supposed to clean the chicken, you massage it, you talk to it a little about how grateful you are for the sacrifice it has made in order to offer you sustenance, you marinate it, you preheat the oven, you toss on some spices, and then you put it in the oven. You might even baste it a little along the way, if you're in the mood.

Point is that you don't just walk in and cook a chicken. You prepare it.

Preparation wins games. Preparation gets you into the college you want, preparation gets you the job you want, and preparation gets you sales. You want to mow lawns or babysit in your neighborhood? You need to be well-prepared. You want to be the best attorney or doctor or engineer in town? You need to prepare. And that preparation starts now.

You want to buy the house of your dreams, get the car of your dreams, and wear the fanciest clothes around? You want to find the most fantastic person in the whole world to marry? Whatever your priorities are—now and later—you can achieve those...with the right preparation.

Do you think you just get to walk up to the guy or girl of your dreams and say, "Hey, uh, so...here I am!" Wrong. This takes preparation and that preparation includes the time you spend getting ready just as much as it does just diving in and learning from your mistakes as we've talked about before. Finding the *right* person to date and marry and spend the rest of your life with means that you're probably going to have to spend a lot of time with a lot of *wrong* persons. And those wrong persons are your preparation for the right person.

Listen, if you are not working hard, if you are not practicing, if you are not preparing—right now—then there is somebody else out there who is. And that person will take your spot at the top of the class. That person will take your starting position on the team. And that person is going to take your job.

What are you doing to prepare for your next event? You know what you want to do—you know that you want better results at school, with your friends, in your business. So, what are you doing, from right now until the moment that event starts, to prepare yourself?

Take heed here, too, because you may often have to get in touch with your own tactics and techniques for physical preparation. There won't always be someone breathing down your back, looking over your shoulder telling you what to do. Take. Control. Of. Your. Own. Preparation. And even if there is someone giving you advice on preparation—someone like a coach or teacher or mentor or parent or band director or the director of a play—even with this advice, you can still go to the next level with your own preparation. Add to what they're saying. Add to their preparation. Your coach has you running and lifting, then you need to work on shooting techniques or passing techniques or pitching techniques—or whatever—on your own time. Your preparation *must* exceed that of your peers around you.

There isn't a single successful professional who doesn't prepare, both mentally and physically, before a game or a meeting or an event.

The best professional speakers have delivered the same talk 100 or 1000 times, and they still have to get themselves into the zone before they take the stage. 1000 times they've been on stage, 1000 times they've told that one story about "their dog and the neighborhood bully and how karma sure is a funny thing, don't ya think?" A thousand times. And they still have to get mentally prepared.

And consider a professional athlete. Do you think they just go out there and just play? They arrive at the stadium, go to the locker room and put on some sneakers and their jersey, and a helmet and Bam! "Let's go play!" Ha. Not quite. They get to the stadium hours early and take time to get to the place where they need to be. Urban Meyer, who has coached football at the University of Florida and *the* Ohio State University said this: he said, "I have yet to be in a game where luck was involved. Well-prepared players make plays. I have yet to be in a game where the most prepared team didn't win."

What a great quote. Well. Prepared. Players. Make. Plays. And that extends to both the mental game and the physical game: both require diligence.

Certainly, there are simpler, more civilian examples, too. Landscapers and bankers, retail associates and store clerks, produce managers and accountants, real estate developers and on and on. All have to prepare for their job and their day before they start. Think about your favorite teacher for a second. Who is your favorite teacher? You think he or she has to prepare mentally every day? Oh, my goodness, yes. Your teacher has to deal—every day—with a group of angels and with a bunch of brats and everything in between. You think they just prepare a few lesson plans, and that's it? No way, José. They've got to be in a pretty special place mentally to deal with those young'ns all day long.

Just like physical preparation, mental preparation starts long before the fans and referees and your mom and dad take their seats in the stands. It starts before your boss walks into your office to check up on your progress on a certain project. It starts *now* and it continues all the way up until game time. Preparation, both mental and physical, is a continuous process.

So, talking about mental preparation, the question, then, is *How*? How do you go about getting mentally prepared? Well, there are many different techniques, and various techniques work for different people. In reality, it's a matter of having *some kind of system*, and then executing that system. What works for you, what gets *you* in the best mode to perform at your peak, to maximize your potential is the system you should be using. Don't worry about other people. Develop your own system of mental preparation.

Some people say that they "aren't very good test takers." What a bunch of bull. Of course you're not a very good test taker. Nobody is a good test taker. Nobody gets excited about taking a test. "Oh, boy! A test? Yes, please. I'll have another, thank you!"

What I can tell you is that half of the battle is won with the attitude you take into it. Half of your preparation for a test mounts on top of strong mental preparation. This is what will put you in a good place for test taking.

If you want to be a better test taker, it is a matter of your mental preparation, just as much as sitting down and studying for hours and hours on end. Do you *need* to study for hours on end? Of course. But you also need to get into the state of mind that, "Hey, I'm getting ready to knock this test out, and *nobody* is going to get in my way!"

The greatest tactic I can give you in order to get into that state of mind is visualization. Visualize, visualize, visualize. This. Is. The. Most. Important. Tactic. Of. Mental. Preparation. Visualize. Put yourself where you want to be.

Visualization starts now, and it is an ongoing process.

And visualization works no matter what you're working on. Visualize the outcome of a test, a meeting, whatever. You can sit down and visualize how you want your entire day to play out. Close your eyes—for two minutes, five minutes, fifteen minutes, however long it takes—and maybe put on a little music, if you'd prefer, and consider how you want that test or that meeting to go.

This is a tactic that athletes use all the time. Like we were just talking about, an athlete doesn't just arrive at the stadium or gym or field, put on a jersey, and go out to play. They arrive early, so they can get to the place they need to be—physically *and* mentally. And this involves visualization. Visualize the moves it takes to get to the basket. Visualize how you are going to stop your defender. Visualize yourself making that pass down field. Visualize your approach to the plate. Visualize yourself standing with a bat, ready to hit the cover off the ball. Visualize the looks on your opponents' faces when you hand them a loss.

Visualization is powerful.

Now, clearly this visualization needs to be backed up by action. In earlier chapters, we've already talked about the need for action to follow your mental preparation. You can want that glass of water across the stage all you want—you can *really* visualize the hydration that it can bring you—but until you walk across stage to pick up that bottle of water, your visualization is basically insignificant.

So, visualization may be only part of the battle, but it is a significant part of the equation here. Physical and mental preparation work hand-in-hand. If you are not mentally focused, if you don't give yourself time ahead of time to relax and zero in on your goal, then you're essentially setting yourself up for failure. Maybe you succeed, maybe you fail, but at least put yourself in a position where you are of the mind to succeed. If you lack focus, if you lack mental discipline, your physical skills matter less and less. I have seen plenty of people go out and outmatch opponents that were much better prepared physically simply because they had a better picture in their mind of how this was going to go down. They centered in on what it was going to take, and they went out and executed.

Think back to David and Goliath. David didn't go in and say, "Eh, well, I reckon I'll give it a shot, see what happens." Ha. Nope. He went in with the determination that he was *going* to take down this giant, and he had a clear cut vision on how that was going to happen. Surely, he had mapped out his plan before he executed it.

Just the same, I've known people who did very well on tests despite lacking intelligence, simply because they had visualized how they were going to tackle this test.

Visualize. Visualize. Visualize. Successful golfers are great at this. They prepare themselves ahead of time for any challenges that could possibly arise on the course. They put themselves on the tee, and they envision shots going in the hole. They think about how they can get those shots in the hole, they think about what they have to do physically to make that happen. And then they visualize how they will feel once they put those shots in the cup.

It's like playing a movie in your head, and then going out and creating that movie.

Mental preparation is a matter of your ability to outline a plan on how you are going to put yourself in victory lane before the competition even starts. The next time you have an event—a test, a game, an important meeting with a teacher or boss or even your parents—visualize how you'd like it to go. Visualize your role in the situation. All of the topics we've talked about already in this book, visualize how you can impact them. Visualize your accountability. Visualize your adaptability to change. Visualize your ability to solve a problem. Visualize your organizational habits.

Visualize. Visualize. Visualize. This works anywhere and everywhere. What do you want to happen? Create it in your mind, and then go create it in reality.

The next step then is to remain mentally strong *throughout* the event—the meeting, the game, the test. Your mental preparation starts before the event and it ends when the event is over. So, what about *during* the event? During the event is when your mental preparation is paramount, because you are *going* to face tough times. Things are not going to go as planned. How will you respond to stressful situations? In some cases, your vision will play out as you would like and in other cases, it won't. So, what are you going to do when it doesn't? Remain mentally strong, and this is where your mental preparation will be important. If you are soundly mentally prepared, you will be much better trained to handle misfortune. If you know it's going to happen—if you know adversity is going to strike, and you have prepared for it—you will be ready to deal with it when it does come.

The point of mental preparation is to get you ready for the good times and the bad times. Mental preparation raises your confidence and lowers your anxiety and negative emotions. If you can accomplish those three things *before* your next event, don't you think you'll be in a pretty great place? If you go into an event with confidence and without stress or negativity, don't you think you're setting yourself up for success?

The counter argument, though, to everything that we're going over is that OVERpreparation can actually be harmful, that we can spend too much time getting ready for an event. Can we over*think* or over*analyze* something? Sure. Many times we spend a ridiculous amount of time with thoughts of "Did I do the right drills? Did I study the right material? Did I read the right books? Did I listen to the right people?" And this can cloud our minds. Of course this is important: you need to be doing the right drills, studying the right material, reading the right books, and listening to the right people...this is all obviously very important. But! Don't over evaluate. Read, do your drills, listen to your mentors, and then just go out and let it all go and perform.

So, to the extent that overthinking or overanalyzing something is overpreparation, then yeah, this can be harmful. I don't know that I've heard of anyone who did too many drills or read too many books or studied too much material. "Ah, yeah, y'know, I really just feel like I worked too hard." False. You can't "work too hard." But you *can* spend so much time overthinking something that you can get inside your own head, and this can be counterproductive. So, quite simply, don't do it. Don't overthink, don't overanalyze. Just prepare, dive in, and learn as you go.

Workbook 12: Supreme Preparation

Key points from this session:

- Preparation starts now. If you are not working hard to prepare, someone else out there is going to take your spot.
- All of the other tools we've been working on throughout this audio program build up to your ability to develop a system for preparation.
- Being prepared means that you can deal with the tough times and capitalize on the good times.
- Being fully prepared means being both *mentally* and *physically* prepared.
    - It's important to lift weights and run and study for tests.
    - It's important to take time to get yourself in the right frame of mind for the upcoming game or test.
    - If you don't have BOTH, though, then you are not fully prepared.
- Games are won long before the coaches and referees take the field. Physical preparation means that you lift and run and practice your skills days, weeks, months, years ahead of time. There are *no* quick fixes.
- You can't count on someone else to show you how to prepare. Take initiative! Your system for mental preparation is YOUR system for mental preparation. Learn from the preparation of others, and make your own system.
- Mental preparation means arriving early and getting yourself into the right state of mind to tackle your next task, be it a game or test.
- For most people, the greatest technique for mental preparation is visualization.
    - Take time to visualize what you want the outcome to be.
    - And then visualize what actions you have to take to make that outcome become reality.
- Preparation requires repetition.

Leadoff question: Preparation is a step that many people either skip or do not emphasize enough when trying to strategize how they can achieve their goals—small or large.

Elaborate below on the most important tactic you were able to take away from this session. How does this apply directly to you?

The ill-prepared: Even when we think that we've done everything we can to prepare, we often fall short. Then, we look back and think, "What could I have done differently?"

This often applies with the imbalance of mental and physical preparation. We do everything we can to prepare physically (hitting the weights, running, and practicing for hours on end), but we don't take time to visualize.

In the space below, discuss a time that you did *everything* you could to prepare, but you still fell short of your goal. In hindsight, what could you have done differently or better? Did your lack of mental preparation play a role in your shortcoming?

12. Supreme Preparation

Your challenges, now! Think about upcoming challenges in your life. Tests, games, family meetings, work, trips, homework. Any genre, any challenge, small or large.

 Below, list the 5 most immediate challenges you are facing (say, within the next week).

1.

2.

3.

4.

5.

Your preparation, now! Now that you understand that preparation is *key* to the success of your challenges, list the 5 ways you can prepare (one by one) for the above challenges.

 (For example, if you're walking into a family meeting, you can visualize how you're going to think win-win on every scenario and how you are going to remain as civil as possible throughout the course of the meeting.)

1.

2.

3.

4.

5.

Your leg up: Whether they act productively or not, most people have some level of understanding about work ethic and problem solving and dealing with failure and rejection and how to effectively set goals and take action.

Supreme preparation, though, takes a little more patience and practice. Joined with these other techniques (sessions), you can do some pretty amazing things.

Pick a mentor. In the next two days, pull them aside (in person or on the phone) and ask them what preparation has meant to them. Ask them a couple of their preparation techniques. Ask them if they are able to see a difference when they prepare ahead of time (both physically and mentally) versus when they arrive at a task unprepared.

Moving forward: So, what now?

Now that you have a much better understanding and grasp on what preparation will mean *specifically* to you (based on what you have learned from others), what will that mean for you as you carry forward into the future? How will you commit to being fully prepared for every challenge that you face? What are you going to do differently?

In the space below, answer these questions by explaining how your supreme preparation will make a positive difference in your life.

Thirteen

When to Lead, and When to Follow

What are you shooting for? That's what I want you to think about here for a second. What are you shooting for? Everything that we are going through is an extension of what you're going after. My biggest request of you, before we get started on this 13th section, is that you have a full grasp on what you're shooting for. We all have tough times. Look at my life. My life is pretty frickin' gravy, but there are times—*many* times per week—that I get frustrated, stressed, sad, angry, and just overall negative about the various issues and conflicts in my life. But the biggest thing that keeps me going is my purpose, my big goals. I am grounded in thinking: "Okay, this is where I'm headed. Now, how do I get there?" If you have a passion, if you have a dream, what else do you need? If you are moving forward toward that passion, toward that dream, then everything matters a little bit less.

Your car has a flat tire.

The power goes out.

Your husband was late to pick up the kids.

It's raining.

You started a new business and no one is buying anything from you.

No one is hiring you.

Regardless of the varying degree of importance placed on these issues, it is crucial to evaluate them—in the moment—and learn from them? You assess these problems, handle them, and move along, move forward. And it is much easier to do this if you have an idea what you're shooting for in the long run.

What's that saying? "Keep your eye on the prize?" If you keep your eye on the prize, if you never lose sight of what you really want, then the good times become more fun, the bad times are easier to manage, and you are less likely to be distracted by negative people who usurp your energy. Keeping your eye on the prize keeps you moving forward. And that's the direction you need to be heading.

I bring all of that up again, because I believe your purpose and your passion in life has a lot of merit in today's discussion on leading and following. After all, if you have a clear picture of what you represent, and you maintain perspective on that direction, then it makes your ability to be a dynamic leader and an effective follower much easier and more efficient. The most important thing is that you are able to balance your responsibilities at the front of the class with taking a step back once in a while, and understanding *when* to do each. You can't lead all of the time, and you can't follow all the time. It just isn't reasonable. It is essential to learn this balance.

Which is why the topic of today's session is *When to Lead, and When to Follow*. In order to best represent ideas on when to lead and when to follow, though, we need to first establish tactics on leadership. After all, if you first know effective means of leadership, then you will be able to grasp when it is important for you to be aggressive and when it is important for you to be a little more passive.

Consider this: I want you to think, for a moment, about the most successful people you know or have heard of. I'm not even going to start naming names, because that would be too random and subjective. Think about *your* current field of interest, though, and think about the people who are most successful. What trait do they all seem to have? Athletes, actors, doctors, lawyers, teachers, corporate executives, and entrepreneurs, what ONE quality do they ALL share?

No, not good looks.

No, not a shiny smile or pretty hair.

No, not lots of money.

No, not a great family, or a great education, or great friends and mentors who helped them along the way, although they may have all of these qualities or none of these qualities.

No, the one quality that ALL successful people have is CHARISMA. They have the ability to walk in a room and be recognized. Maybe they light up the room or maybe not; maybe they're good looking or maybe they're not; maybe they come from great pedigree and maybe not; BUT! They *all* have their own style, their own way of being.

Now, having charisma doesn't have one linear meaning. Charisma doesn't necessarily mean being the guy or gal who just gets along with *everybody*, who is liked by everybody, who walks through the halls and everybody turns their heads to see what a cool person they have in their midst. "Oh, my. What charisma he has. Look at him walking the halls. With all of that charisma."

Not necessarily true.

Charisma comes from one thing: confidence. Charisma starts with confidence and branches from there. When you watch a talk show or see an interview on the news, charismatic people always act like they know *exactly* what they're talking about, like they have it all figured out. Maybe they do—in many cases they do—but not always. But that's not important. They act as though they are unimpressed with the world. *Their* style is *their* charisma. Their demeanor is their charisma.

What I mean by this is that successful people understand—and 100% believe in—what they're doing. Of course they care about other people and they mind what others are saying about them, but at the end of the day, their charisma is an extension of their fervent belief in their potential. That is charisma. And charisma is a major force of leadership.

Are all successful people leaders? Not necessarily. But all charismatic people have the potential to be leaders. They can choose to enact that power or not, but charisma equals leadership.

What I'm telling you is that charisma can be taught. Confidence can be taught. You aren't born with a cool walk and a cute laugh. You aren't born with the ability to work a room and hold conversations with anyone and everyone. These traits are learned, and whether you choose to use these superpowers, it's important to at least have them in your toolbox.

The question is: Are leaders born or made? They're made. And that creation—the making of a leader—takes care, precision, persistence, and a willingness to continually learn what is necessary in order to get to that next level. When someone says that leaders are made and not born, they are saying that leaders take the time and due diligence to get where they'd like to get through hard work, discipline, accountability, good problem solving techniques, etcetera, etcetera. Everything we've been talking about, all the lessons we've been learning throughout the course of this book add up to an effective leader.

Do you want to be a leader? Well, studies show that success comes easier for leaders, but even if you don't have the desire to be a leader, maybe it still makes sense to understand the techniques and tactics required to be a leader. At the very least, hold the option to be a leader, and then you have the ability to make the decision to step back if you'd like. From there, you can make the decision to what extent you would like to exercise your leadership powers, so to speak, but *you* get to make that choice. By having the ability to lead, *you* get to make that decision on how and when you're going to lead rather than the decision being made for you if you have no idea what you're doing.

So, to recap what we have so far: One, your charisma is YOUR charisma. Two, this charisma comes from the environment that you choose and your ability to drink in the world around you, learn from the successes of those who have made it, and the failures of those who have not.

Now, when is the most effective time to follow? After all, we're talking about a balance here, a balance between leading and following, and if you know when to do each, you will be a powerful component to whatever it is you're working on, whether it's something individual or in a group and whether it's a major project, a long-term goal, or just a mini assignment.

When you don't know something or you don't have an answer, follow. This is a major downfall for many people. Overleading. Trying to lead too much. They just like to be in the front, they just like to be in control, they just like to hear themselves talk. This can be detrimental and can ruin your reputation.

The ability to follow is just as—if not *more*—important than your ability to follow. Does that make sense? This is a valuable lesson, a lesson I learned the hard way, much later than I would have liked. I obviously don't live my life with regret—none of us should live our lives with regret—but if there's *one* tactic I could have used in my toolbox when I was younger, it is the ability to know how to follow.

I learned this late. I always wanted to be at the front of the class; the head of the project; the captain of the team; the leader of the group. But mostly, what I did was talk too much. I spent so much time in front of everybody, talking and acting like I was a leader, when I could have stepped back for a moment, every now and then at least, and *listened*.

See what you're working with. Acknowledge your talents. What. Are. You. Good. At? And what talents are you best left to delegate? Delegation is *the* characteristic of effective leaders. THE characteristic. All leaders know how to delegate, know how to pass along tasks that they each don't want to do or are incapable of doing. Pass it up to someone who does know what they're doing, and follow them.

Delegation is surveying your team and deciding who is most capable of completing which tasks. It's not being bossy or merely assigning tasks. Delegation is empowerment. You're saying, "I believe in your capabilities to perform this task better than anyone else can, and certainly better than I can on my own." Don't just assign a task. Delegate it. Empower someone.

Effective delegation is oh-so-important for being an effective leader. Delegation is all part of your ability, as a leader, to follow, to listen, and to say, "I don't know what is going on here, and I need help. I need to learn." I mean, think about this: even if you are confident and charismatic, as many successful people are, don't you see value in your ability to listen, to absorb, to, as we discussed previously, surround yourself with a group of people who can help you take your life where you want it to go.

And besides, someone who can effectively delegate a task, someone who can effectively organize a team to all work together toward one common goal, is freeing up *a lot* of time to spend doing other, perhaps more important things, or at least those things at which he or she excels. If you can delegate, then you can focus on where your attention is best suited.

This. Is. Leadership. The ability to follow is also an effective means of leadership. An effective leader knows when to hop to the front of their team at work, and they know when to reel back and listen. Leaders have both the capability to lead and to follow, and they know when to do both.

Just because you're not the quarterback or the vice president doesn't mean you can't be a leader. Most leaders—at least the very effective ones—lead by example. You don't have to be the loudest or strongest. You *do* have to be the one who dives on the floor for a loose ball, who stays after practice to take some extra pitches, and who gets to practice early in order to work on your serve. You have to be the one who gets that powerpoint presentation to your boss ahead of schedule and exceeding her expectations; to be the one to provide your clients with more than they asked for. Leadership doesn't have to be vocal. Leadership is a matter of you *showing* your winning qualities just as much as it is *talking* about your winning qualities.

Do you understand this? Do you see what I'm talking about here? Lead. By. Example. There are times to be vocal and there are times to stay silent. Learn these techniques. Learn what you have to do to be the most effective member of the organization that you can be. Lead. By. Example. Less talk, more walk.

And as such, you can even turn from a follower to a leader without even knowing it. If you do what you're told, as you're told, and you do it better than everyone else, people will notice. They will want to emulate you. They will flock to you. Following becomes leading. Sometimes it's okay just to keep your mouth shut and work hard. Think outside the box and apply your own ideas to a task, but that doesn't mean that you have to take center stage every time.

Balance. Your. Ability. To. Lead. And. Your. Ability. To. Follow.

When you are able, lead; when you aren't, follow.

When you are the prescribed expert, lead; when you don't know much about the subject matter, follow.

When you have an established track record, lead; when you are a rookie, follow.

When you have great, actionable ideas, lead; when you don't, follow.

If you know the answer, lead; if you have something to learn, follow.

When you are in a position of power, lead (and delegate); when you are at the bottom, follow.

When people are counting on you, lead; when people don't know you, follow.

And on and on. I'm confident you could make up twenty examples on the distinction between leading and following. The point is that *your ability to follow will nourish your ability to one day lead.*

So, then, let me ask you this question: What happens when you "over lead", when you spend more time talking than listening? Micromanaging, that's what happens. And you *don't* want to be a micromanager. You start to over-scrutinize the work of the people around you. Micromanaging happens when you are trying too hard to lead. You are spending too much time leading when you *could and should* be taking a step back. You could easily fall into this path of micromanaging.

You don't want this. Your peers won't respect you. Your subordinates won't respect you; your employees won't respect you. You'll start to lose them. You'll start to lose customers. Micromanaging is ineffective. Overleading is ineffective.

Do you need to pay attention to your business, to your life, to your affairs, and to your projects? Of course. But you also need to have confidence in those around you. There is a fine balance here of managing and stepping back to listen, to letting the business or group project run itself.

Empower. Delegate authority. Don't stand over your flock and tell them what to do. Keep an eye out, but don't monitor *every* move. Show them what to do, and allow them to do it. There is a time to lead, and there is a time to follow. Learn the difference.

In front of the class or at the back?

As the vocal leader of your team or the silent assassin?

As the lead on the stage or behind the scenes?

Where are you most effective? Think about this. Don't micromanage. Don't overlead. Instead, delegate. Empower.

When to lead, and when to follow. What we know is that it is possible to learn to have the power to lead, to delegate tasks, to empower people to outperform. And you can do this whether you are in the front of the class or the back, whether you have incredible skills or no skills, and whether you have the loudest voice or no voice at all. You have the potential to lead, and you have the ability to follow. Your success—the college you get into, the number of games you win, the number of happy clients on your roster—all of these things are a result of your understanding of and your ability to lead and your understanding of and your ability to follow.

Workbook 13: When to Lead, and When to Follow

---•∽⊰⊱∾•---

Key points from this session:

- If you have a clear picture of what you represent, and you ALWAYS have perspective on that direction, then it makes your ability to be a dynamic leader and to be an effective follower much easier and more efficient.
- Anybody can take the stage and attempt to lead. And anyone can sit in the corner and be a follower. The trick is to know *when* to do each.
- The number one quality that ALL successful people have is charisma.
    - They aren't necessarily tall or good-looking and they may or may not come from a certain pedigree.
    - But they have their own style; their own way of being.
    - Charisma—and by extension, the ability to lead or follow—is a matter of confidence.
- Leaders are made; not born. Great leaders learn from the world around them, both the successes and the failures.
- Follow first, and then learn how to lead.
    - Your ability to follow is just as important as your ability to lead. Learn to do both, and learn how to balance them.
    - Don't over-lead! Nobody likes a micromanager.
    - If you are an expert and the best man or woman for the job and you have great ideas and you've proven yourself, lead. If you are not the expert and someone else is better for the job, follow.
    - Learn and understand your role as either a leader or a follower, depending on the circumstances of each scenario.
- Delegation is surveying your team and deciding who is most capable of completing which tasks.
- Lead by *showing* rather than *talking*. Lead by example.

Leadoff question: As you move through the rest of your days in school and then on to the professional world, you have the capability to be an incredible leader *if* you can learn how to balance leadership with the ability to follow.

What is the number one thing you were able to take away from this session, something that you didn't fully understand before? Elaborate a little here. (Don't just say, "Well, I learned that you need to balance leading and following.") What is one specific example from this session that will work for you NOW and as you move forward into the future?

Hindsight being 20/20: The point of every session we're going through here is to grow, to look back and improve on your past mistakes and look forward to take actionable steps for success.

Think back to a time when you neglected to lead when you should have or you were following and you wish you would have stepped up to the plate to assume a leadership role.

Briefly describe the event, and then briefly discuss how you will handle the issue differently next time.

The leaders around you: Every successful person is not necessarily a leader and every leader is not necessarily successful. These two characteristics are not always 100% compatible, even if they might run in alignment from time to time.

Moreover, as you now know, leaders follow when appropriate and lead when appropriate.

Think about a leader in your life who you know personally: a teacher, a principal, a business owner, a coach, a local politician. Below, list five characteristics that you think help to make them the leader that they are.

Then, below that, list two or three times when it is important—in their line of work, specifically—for them to assume the role of a follower.

Name and title of leader:

5 leadership characteristics:

1.

2.

3.

4.

5.

Times he or she needs to follow:

1.

2.

3.

A time to lead: Now that you have a better idea of when to lead and when to follow, talk about the next situation where you will have the opportunity to lead. It could be tomorrow, next week, or next month. It could be on the playing field, in the classroom, or at a meeting at work.

What is your next opportunity to lead?

A time to follow: Conversely, being a leader is also a matter of knowing when it is time to follow.

Discuss below the next opportunity you will have to follow rather than lead. In fact, this could even be a time when you really want to lead or even a time when you think you're the best person to be the leader, but you know that it is best for you to take a backseat role.

What is your next opportunity to follow?

Fourteen

Building an Outstanding Team Around You

All of this work, all of your studying and effort here with *Next Level Success*, and the biggest news I can report to you is this: you are not going to accomplish your success on your own. Write that down in your notebook, and tattoo it on your belly. You are *not* going to accomplish your success alone. Sure, it's a little hypocritical of me to say this after all of these chapters devoted to your distinctive and solitary advancement, but it's important to acknowledge both that you can do great things solo *and* you must look elsewhere for support. Most of what we've been talking about, after all, revolves around your ability to accomplish things on your own, to be successful on your own. Being accountable. Having a strong work ethic. Solving problems. Living with passion. Leading. Following. Having the courage to be different. And on and on. These are tactics that you can—and should—work on, on an individual level. Grow from within, take care of yourself first. And then go out and find like-minded people. Find. People. To. Work. With. Make a difference in someone else's life, as we were talking about in the session on having the courage to be different. Remember? It's all reciprocated, right? When you make a difference in someone else's life, the theory—and often the reality—is that they will be able to make a difference in your life as well.

This is a powerful concept, this is the *core* of teamwork, and this is the core of what you can be doing to take your life to the next level. This idea is based on your ability to compile a group of worthy people to be part of your team, a team with whom you can climb to the next level *together*.

I mean, think about it. Think about this: when you "make it", when you reach these great heights for which you're aiming, do you want to be standing up there alone? You climb Everest, isn't it kind of lonely to be there by yourself? You get an award, don't you want to have people with you who you can thank? You earn a big raise or get into the #1 college of your choice, don't you want to share that with someone?

It's fun going to a movie by yourself sometimes, but don't you also want someone there with you with whom you can discuss it afterwards?

There is, obviously, great power in individual achievement, but, at times, don't you want to have someone standing by your side? "We" did this instead of "I" did this. In recalling my greatest accomplishments—victories on the basketball court, books published, speeches I've done, awards I've received, various major media appearances—in each of those situations, there was *always* somebody there with me. Maybe it was my mom or dad, or maybe it was a friend or my wife, or maybe it was someone with whom I had shared a vision. A teammate; a colleague; a partner on a project; workmates; aides; coaches; and compatriots.

Think about this for yourself. Think about the cool things you've accomplished. Think about the cool things you've done. Was somebody there with you? Did somebody help you? Or maybe you went at it alone? Do you think you could have done more with the help of others?

Seriously, think about this. Think about your last great accomplishment. Did you do everything on your own? Perhaps you pride yourself on being an independent person, but surely, someone was there to help you along the way, no? A parent, a teacher, a mentor, a manager, a friend, a coach. Someone was most assuredly there, on some level. How did they aid your success? And perhaps, a better question is, what more could you have accomplished with additional assistance? You did *this much* on your own; now, how much *more* could you have done with a little guidance?

Build. An. Outstanding. Team. Around. You. Start with yourself first—be responsible for your individual accomplishments—and then build from there. You'll be happier, healthier, and wiser, but most importantly, you have a chance at a new level of success. As an individual, you can do great things. And with great people around you, you can do even greater things.

I mean, think about the great championship teams in sports history. Pick a team sport. Any team sport. Basketball, baseball, softball, volleyball, football, soccer, synchronized swimming...any team sport. Those teams do not win without quality team members. Yeah, sure, some players are more talented, but every player has a role on that team, right?

And the same goes for individual pursuits: golf, tennis, a solo singing career. Even these individual pursuits require coaches and trainers and a support group to make success possible.

Chemistry. No matter the venue—from the classroom to the court to the boardroom—chemistry is the dividing factor between a good team and a great team. *Outstanding teams have chemistry.*

The USA Women's softball team won 3 Olympic Gold Medals in a row—3 OLYMPIC GOLD

MEDALS IN A ROW!—because they knew how to play well together. They gelled. They had chemistry.

Outstanding. Teams. Have. Chemistry.

GE and Adidas and Wal-Mart and any other business behemoth got where they are now because the leaders built strong teams around them who knew what they had to do to succeed.

And the same it is with you and the team you are part of, whether it is a group project or a sports team or a business venture, or even your family or a romantic relationship. Your team needs to have chemistry. Whether you are a leader or a follower, whether you join a team or are the orchestrator of the formation of a team, it doesn't matter. The teams you are a part of—the team you build around you—will enjoy success, or not, based on the level of chemistry that exists between you and them.

Do you have chemistry with the people around you? If so, great. If not, how can you fix that?

Now, what should we be thinking about when we build a team around us? Well, lots of things, but for one, we should build a team so we can emulate success. Think about what success looks like to you, and then think about who can help you get there.

Who can expedite that process?

They don't have to be close friends. Listen, your team doesn't have to be a team of people with whom you have contact *every* day. They can be, sure, they can be friends or daily acquaintances, but your team could also be a series of singular encounters, perhaps, individuals who you meet once or twice and never see again. Or your team can be comprised of non-acquaintances who you see on a regular basis.

They can be mentors that you take out to lunch, for example. Actually, this is a *great* technique for you to adhere to. Take people out to lunch. I love doing this. I love getting together with people for lunch, and I always take something away. Even if I go to lunch with someone and they turn out to be a bonehead, I take something away from that encounter. "Okay, now I know what it means to be a bonehead." For every bonehead I meet, there are ten great lunches or dinners or other encounters where I'm able to take great things away, really learn a lot. I have learned so much from the people around me, above me, from these singular encounters with people who are where I want to be.

So, who am I talking about arranging these meetings with? Well, the simple answer is anybody who is more successful than you, which, for most of us, is *a lot* of people. Like, a ton of people.

A longer answer, though, is to take a look at the people in fields you are interested in. Maybe you don't know what you want to do next with your life, and you'd like some perspective. The best way to do that is to shake hands with and speak with people in all of a variety of fields in order to gain some insight into their world. What their lives are like. What *they* did to get where they are now. These people are—right now—where you want to be later. You're trying to get where they are, and perhaps beyond.

Take them out to lunch.

Take them out for coffee.

Take them out for a strawberry banana smoothie.

Take them out to dinner.

This is a great investment of your time and money. *Learn from those who have succeeded before you.* This is your team of mentors, and mentors need to be a part of your outstanding team just as much as your friends and family and the group with whom you're working on a project. Build your outstanding team as you'd like your team to look. After all, your team—this outstanding team that you are building—is going to be comprised of people you see every day and people you see maybe once in your entire life.

Now, your team. The question is: Who are you choosing to be part of your team, your permanent team?

I read a study recently—a 20-year study of 5,000 people—and this study found one simple conclusion: if you surround yourself with happy people, you will be happy yourself. That's it. If you surround yourself with happy people, you will be happy yourself. Makes sense, doesn't it? I mean, think about the last time you were in a group of negative, pessimistic people, Debbie Downers or Billy Buzzkills. Their attitudes were contagious, weren't they? You started to feel a little negative, a little down, too, didn't you? Sure you did. Even the most positive among us, even those of us who have such jovial, happy spirits, we can be easily distracted and easily manipulated by the company we keep. I'm telling you: if you surround yourself with negative people, if you build a team of pessimists, you will gradually become more pessimistic yourself.

And conversely, if you surround yourself with happy people, you will gradually become a happier person.

This one technique, as simple as it is, can make a huge impact on your life. If you don't take anything else away from this chapter today, take away the fact that your success is an extension of the people you have around you, and the people you have around you is *your choice*. Surround yourself with happiness, and you will be happy. Surround yourself with negativity, and you will start to walk around with a scowl on your face all the time. And this will lead to a wrinkly face and anger and depression and a whole host of problems that won't serve you well later in your life.

I read another study recently that happier people are more successful people. This study showed graphs and statistics and even income ranges of various people's success levels matched up with their happiness. They were showing that the happier somebody is, the more successful they are. No, it isn't the other way around: it isn't that the more successful they are, the happier they are. Happiness comes first. And then success. And then more happiness. But it starts with your desire to be happy and to figure out how to make yourself that way *regardless* of where you are in life—how much money you have, how nice your car is, what college you get into. Happiness starts now. Are you with me here?

And a good way to start learning to be happy is to surround yourself with happy people.

So, you put together these two studies I read recently, and what do you get: Okay, well, for one, happiness is an extension of the people around you—family, friends, teachers, mentors, coaches—your team. And happy people are more successful people. So, if you want to be more successful, you need to be happier, and if you want to be happier, you need to surround yourself with happy people.

Be happy, be successful. Make yourself happy; make yourself successful.

In the end, it is proven that the people you surround yourself with are a representation of the success that you will enjoy.

The key word here in the title of this chapter is *outstanding*. You don't want to build a mediocre team. A mediocre team gets in the way. A mediocre team is going to have negative consequences; you might as well work alone. You don't want to build a "pretty good" team; and you don't want to aim to build a team that is good-looking or a team that has nice clothes or a team full of people who have really pretty teeth.

You want to build an *outstanding* team. You want a team that is ready to work when it's appropriate and ready to play when it's appropriate, and you want a team that is ready to get results. You want a team that *gets it done.*

The thing is that these people, these truly quality people are a dime a dozen. They aren't necessarily easy to find; they aren't around every corner. Which makes it even more important for you to really put in the work to recruit and maintain these outstanding people. Your outstanding team starts with finding outstanding individuals, and your outstanding team starts with you putting in work to *manage* that team.

Put in the work to build a team, and put in the work to keep that team.

Now, all of this is important, but the most effective way to build a strong team is to *get results on an individual basis first*. Then, you will be able to choose who you want to have on your team. If you are following everything else we've been talking about, if you are succeeding and dealing with failure with your head up and being accountable and solving problems, then people will come to you. *You* will be the guy or gal who people want to work with. I'm telling you this as a fact. Word of mouth will spread—positive or negative—and if that word of mouth is positive, then people are going to want to be a part of your life.

If you are getting results, if you are showing the world that you mean business, that you are fun, that you are an achiever, that you are consistently on the brink of success, then your team will be much easier to build around you.

And from there, magic can happen. What you can accomplish with a strong team, whether your team is two people or twenty people, what you can accomplish with a quality team is boundless; limitless; vast; immeasurable.

But this is *your* responsibility. Do you understand that? Great things can happen and those great things are in *your* hands. Work hard and develop a quality reputation on an individual level, and then go out to pick the quality team that you would like to be part of.

Surround. Yourself. With. Outstanding. People. And your life will escalate to the next level.

Workbook 14: Building an Outstanding Team Around You

Key points from this session:

- YOU ARE NOT GOING TO ACCOMPLISH YOUR SUCCESS ALONE.
  - Your success comprises your ability to make positive, productive moves on your own, and then...
  - surround yourself with positive, productive people.
- Teams don't win championships without quality team members, from top to bottom.
  - Chemistry is the dividing factor between a *good* team and a *great* team.
  - You don't always get to choose your team. So your ability to compromise, to work with the team you've been dealt, is important.
- Who can help you get where you want to get?
  - Take successful people out to lunch and pick their brains.
  - Networking—and the exchange of information with various people—will be HUGE to your future success.
- If you surround yourself with happy people, you will be happy yourself.
- And the happier you are *now*, the more successful you will become *later*. (This is a fact! Remember the studies?)
- Life is better when you have someone to share it with.
- If you work hard to get results as an individual, your quality team will come to you. If you build your own life first, your quality team will follow.

Leadoff question: In reviewing your notes from session 14, what is the ONE big thing you learned? What is your ONE big takeaway? (This can be a story, a lesson, a tactic, a call to action, or, well…anything.) Spend a paragraph or so elaborating on what this meant SPECIFICALLY to you:

Positive characteristics of *your* team: It's one thing to hear someone else talk about the positive characteristics of his or her team, but what does *your* team look like? List five or six qualities that you look for in the people you add to your team:

14. Building an Outstanding Team Around You

Analyzing your current team: This is important! Let's take a look at your current team. List below the three top members of your team (outside of your family). These can be positive or negative members; friends your age or mentors; people you've chosen to be part of your team or people on your team that you didn't elect to work with.

List their name and then list the positive attributes they bring to the table. Finally, list one additional thing you'd like to get from that team member.

Name:
Positive Characteristics:

One additional thing you'd like to get from that team member:

Name:
Positive Characteristics:

One additional thing you'd like to get from that team member:

Name:
Positive Characteristics:

One additional thing you'd like to get from that team member:

As tough as it is, there comes a time when you have to "trim the fat" and work to cut out—or at least minimize the time you spend with—members of your team. In your mind, answer:

Are the people above productive members of your team? Is this a *net positive* for you? Or, do you need to work to cut them out, so you can spend time with the more positive members of your team?

If you'd like to continue working with these team members (assuming you have a choice), what can *you* do to take action on the "one additional thing you'd like to get from that team member"?

Taking action on building your team: There are two aspects of building a great team: *creation* and *maintenance*. First, you have to find quality members of your team, and then you have to work to maintain those relationships.

So, we're going to do two things here:

First, think about one person who you would like to be part of your team (who isn't already). What can you do NOW to take action on making him or her part of your team?

Second, think about what you can be doing to maintain your team. Call one of the four people from page 3 and tell them, "Hey, I value you as part of my team. What can I be doing to be a more positive, productive member of your team?" Communication is important, and this will allow you to develop a quality relationship with the team members around you.

Fifteen
On Remaining Humble

Here you are, on the verge of representing superhuman powers. Over the next year, two years, five years, ten years, with the tools you acquire from reading books and listening to your mentors and otherwise learning from the world around you, you are going to accomplish *amazing* things. This is a fact. Keep tabs on what you've learned here in *Next Level Success* and elsewhere, and you are going to do great things. I'm telling you. Everyone will flock to you, and everyone will want to emulate your success.

But! And again, this is a big "but", the question is: Can you handle that success? Do you know how to compose yourself in both defeat *and* victory? It's one thing to handle rejection and failure, but can you handle success? And can you handle success *with grace*? Can you take your winnings and build on those winnings, or are you going to squander them by being arrogant and greedy and burning bridges?

You will win, and so will people remember you as a gracious, classy winner or as a sleazy, greedy, inconsiderate one?

Humility. This is the mark of the truly successful person, the truly revered person. You don't just want success; you want people to admire you. And people will admire you if you maintain a level of modesty.

If you are humble, it doesn't matter whether you're successful or not, people will admire you; they will respect you; they will speak highly of you; they will speak kindly of you; and they will want to be around you.

Be humble *first*, and the success will follow. Then, no matter what, when that success does come, you will be prepared to handle it with grace. I'm telling you, there is nothing worse than seeing someone—on TV or in person—accepting an award or winning a championship and them having their time in the sun and taking that time to be braggadocious.

You should go lookup Michael Jordan's Hall of Fame speech. I'm sure you can find it online somewhere. Check YouTube. Everything's on YouTube. I lost my wallet the other day, and I found it on YouTube. Here is Michael Jordan, the greatest basketball player of all-time—I don't care what generation you're reading this, he *is* the greatest basketball player of all time—and he goes up on stage to receive the amazing honor of being inducted into the basketball hall of fame, and for fifteen minutes or so, he basically talks trash about a bunch of people, thanks a few people, and then he gets off stage. How arrogant is that? The greatest basketball player of all time doesn't have a trace of humility.

How sad is that?

You want to win, and you want to be respected as a person for that win. Plenty of people win, and plenty of people are admired for their talent, but not all of them are respected.

With humility, you can win *and* you can be respected.

How does a humble person act?

There are many, many, many, MANY characteristics of the humble person, and there's no way that I could break down the anatomy of someone who walks with humility. Indeed, humble people can be found in many different forms, so for me to sit here and start naming all of these characteristics wouldn't make sense, and frankly, it wouldn't do much good, since you need to represent your *own* persona, your *own* humility, your *own* stature of success, right? Be your own person. But! There are four characteristics that every successful, humble person represents. And that's what we're going to focus on here. Beyond these four, there are certainly more, but these four are at the core of humility, so if you intend to be respected for your success rather than having people talking about you behind your back; if you intend to attract people to you rather than repel them; and if you want your success to multiply rather than remain stagnant, these four core characteristics of humility are imperative. After all, succeeding at something is one thing; *continuing* to succeed is sometimes the challenge. And that challenge can be answered with humility.

Okay, so, four things:

Number one: be accountable for your actions. I'm not going to elaborate on this, because we did an entire chapter on it. Suffice to say, own your triumphs and your setbacks: when you screw up, raise your hand and take responsibility. Likewise, when you do well, pat yourself on the back.

Simple enough.

Number two: always say thank you. Always. *Always* be grateful. Just like we talked about before, it's important to recognize those who have helped you get where you are now. As independent as you may be, you didn't get here on your own. Somebody or a bunch of somebodies helped you, right? Isaac Newton said, "If I have seen further than others, it is by standing upon the shoulders of giants." Think about that for a second: If I have seen further than others, it is by standing upon the shoulders of giants. No matter where you are, someone helped you get there.

So, what do you do? *Show gratitude.* This is appreciating where you come from, and this is being humble.

Now, as we've talked about, there are a thousand ways to say "thanks", so it doesn't matter which course you take. An email, a phone call, a handshake, a gift, flowers, a box of chocolate. Simple or extravagant, doesn't matter. Gratitude is gratitude. But make it meaningful.

A handwritten card goes a long way. And so does a nice crayon drawing. You're never too old to send someone a handwritten card or a crayon drawing.

And in many cases, looking someone in the eye, and saying, "I really appreciate what you did for me," can be more profound and more appreciated than sending someone flowers or chocolates.

However you do it, make it meaningful.

Tactic number three is a simple one: Smile. That's it. No one likes some dude or girl who is growling. If you're a jerk, then people will quickly form a negative opinion of you. If you're whiny, people won't want to be around you. If you are not approachable, well, people won't approach you.

But if you smile, if you give off the aura that you are harmless and endearing, then you will go a lot farther. Remember our talk on happiness? Happiness isn't necessarily success or having nice things or name-dropping all of your important friends. "Oh, I tell you, I just had dinner with the governor. Oh, what a mau-velous time we had." No. Happiness is surrounding yourself with happy people, and surrounding yourself with happy people starts with your smile.

This relates to humility in that a smile means that you aren't acting like you are above everyone else. Don't ever—no matter how successful you are—don't *ever* act like you're above someone else. I just read a quote by the great French thinker and social commentator Charles de Montesquieu. He said: "To be truly great, one has to stand *with* people, not above them." Think about that for a second. To be truly great, one has to stand *with* people, not above them.

And a great way to do this is to be inviting. And often, the way to do this is to smile. A smile neutralizes your ego. Someone who is scowling or grimacing isn't inviting the world to them, and this often means that they think they deserve better, that they aren't satisfied with what they have, that they are mad at the world for whatever reason.

So, smile. I mean, I know you aren't an angry person—most people are generally cordial—but I'm telling you to take your smile to the next level, to really accentuate that you are a happy person, to really extend warmth to those around you.

Your smile doesn't have to be fake or contrived. Just find things to smile about. Appreciate what you have. This is a mark of humility: appreciating what you have. Maybe you live in a two-bedroom townhouse with six people or maybe you have your own room in a big house with a pool in the backyard. Whatever kind of life you are living, you are reading this book right now, you are alive, and so there is surely something for you to be grateful about.

If you are giving off this aura that you appreciate what you have, then you are giving off an aura of humility. And this humility will double, triple, quadruple your success.

The fourth and final characteristic of humility? A humble person *never* rests on their success. Just as a humble person appreciates where they come from, a humble person is also never fully satisfied with their station in life. Never stop working, learning, and growing. Never stop moving forward. Never stop taking your life to the next level. Listen, you are going to do great things. I'm *telling* you that you are going to do great things. But don't rest on that. Don't ever say, "What I've accomplished is good enough." Always appreciate what you have, what you've done, what you've accomplished. Always take a moment to stop and smell the roses. You should always be proud of the fruits of your labor.

But! Always strive for more. Greed can be good at times, if you manage it effectively and if you're not cheating your fellow man. You can want more. That's okay. The question, then, is not, "What *have* you accomplished?" The question is, "What are you *going* to accomplish?"

And that's what being humble is all about: the next step. The next level is always *right there*, ready for the taking. And what it takes is your commitment to always be learning, always be asking questions, and always be focused. Listen! Humble people don't lose focus. They don't win a game and then go out and celebrate by being a fool on the streets. Humble people win, enjoy it with their family and friends, have some cheese fries and a Coca Cola, and then they go about figuring out how they can win the next one.

- They get an "A" and they figure out how they can get another "A".
- They get into the college of their choice and they figure out how they can maximize this forthcoming education rather than just thinking, "Well, I already got in, so I'm good."
- They get a promotion and they figure, "Well, this is an honor. Now, how can I make the most of this opportunity?"

Remaining humble includes continuing your education. You're never "there". You've always got work to do. So, keep moving forward:

Read books.

Listen to audio programs.

Take your mentors out to lunch.

Do it all. Take time to understand that you are great at what you do, and you can always be widening your scope.

Humble. People. Are. Always. Striving. For. The. Next. Level. Regardless of what kind of success or failure they have come upon, humble people remain on the hunt.

15. On Remaining Humble

Be accountable.
Say thank you.
Smile.
And *never stop learning*.

Humility is practicing random acts of kindness without worrying about taking credit.

You don't have to talk to your friends about how much money you donated to a certain cause; you don't have to post pictures about all of the service you're doing; you don't have to stroke your own ego or seek congratulations.

Yeah, of course it feels good to get together for a nice dinner to celebrate your graduation from middle school or a big exam you conquered. There are always times to be prideful. But I'm just saying that maybe humility is keeping some things to yourself. Next time you do perform a great deed for yourself, try keeping it to yourself.

Practice random acts of kindness without worrying about receiving credit.

And while you're at it, it's important to understand that there's no sense trying to one-up people. They say something, and you feel the need to say something *better* that *you* did. Chill. It's okay to stay back in the shadows a little bit. You can do great things, and you can just mosey on along as if nothing happened.

Even if you're the champ, you don't necessarily have to say, "Yeah, I'm the champ." Deflect the praise elsewhere: your trainers, your coaches, your teachers, your parents, your teammates. Give the credit to others FIRST. Your credit comes from your performance, right?

Some of these ideas that we're talking about, these ideas on humility, might parallel with the ideas on toughness from Chapter 11. Because think about it, if you are tough, if you are secure, then there is no other way to be than humble, right? Humility is confidence. Humility is accountability. And humility is toughness. Humility isn't easy. It's easy to tell everybody how great you are— "Oh, look at me!"—but it takes a tough person to step back and acknowledge faults or to take the time to say, "Hey, thank you for all you do."

It takes a tough and humble person to say, "Hey, I screwed up."

It takes a tough and humble person to find something to smile about when times are going very well.

It takes a tough and humble person to keep learning, even when we all know we have it all figured out. We're all convinced that we know everything and that we've got it all figured out, so it takes a tough person to say, "I really want to keep learning." *That* is humility.

Be tough; be humble.

Also, think about this: How great is it to be able to look back at where you came from? How exciting is it to have humble beginnings? Pretty great, right? I mean, this, right now—these, right now—are the good old days. This is where you come from.

One day, you're going to be 80 years old, sitting on a porch, sipping lemonade, probably wearing a diaper, and you are going to smile about the memories you have of where you came from.

You don't want to be handed anything. You want to earn it. And moreover, when you look back on these days—whether you are 13 years old, 17, 35, 55, 70, or 90 years old—when you look back on these days, you will want to be grateful that you appreciated these days, that wherever you came from, you appreciated what you had, you took success in stride, and you were always kind to people.

This is what humility is all about. Look back on these days and be grateful that you appreciated your life. And the only thing you can do *right now* is just that: appreciate your life. Take success in stride. Be kind.

The crazy thing is that greatness doesn't necessarily parallel your ego. Some arrogant people achieve greatness, and some humble people don't ever achieve a single great thing in their lives. There's no way to measure any kind of correlation between success or failure and humility or arrogance.

But we can measure humility against other factors. You will be happier, you will be more respected, and you will be more poised to capitalize on the little bits and pieces of success that are sure to come.

Are you going to do great things? Yes, you are. I can say that with conviction.

The question then is, how are you going to handle that next level of success?

Workbook 15: On Remaining Humble

Key points from this session:

- Humility is the mark of the truly successful person. It's one thing to enjoy success on the back of all of the other sessions we've gone through.
    - But what's most important is how you handle that success.
    - Will people remember you as a gracious, classy winner or as a sleazy, greedy, inconsiderate one?
- If you're humble, people will respect you regardless of whether you are successful or not.
- Being humble means representing four characteristics:
    1. Accountability for your actions: it's not easy to say, "Hey, I screwed up on that one."
    2. Gratitude: always say "thank you".
    3. Smile.
    4. Never rest on your success.
- Work *with* people rather than trying to *challenge* them or "one-up" them.
- The difference between someone who is appreciated for what they do and someone who is not appreciated for what they do is that someone who carries arrogance with them is not loved; not respected; not appreciated.

Leadoff question: Humility is important no matter what scale of success you have enjoyed. Small-time to big-time, your humility is a representation of who you are and how much respect you will receive.

After reading this 15th and final chapter, what is your one big takeaway on humility? What is the one tactic or story or call to action that you carry forward from this session?

Your arrogance, then: Representing humility isn't just a switch that you turn on or off. It is within the fabric of your being. It will require practice and repetition rather than a quick fix.

Think back, for a moment, to a time when you represented arrogance. Of course you're not an arrogant person, but we always slip up and show some level of arrogance at some point. In this situation, what were the circumstances? How did you act? What could you have done differently?

15. On Remaining Humble

The arrogance around you: You are surrounded by both humble people and arrogant people. Some you respect, and some you don't.

Think about someone you know (in your real life, not on TV) who represents arrogant characteristics. How are they viewed by your peers? Are they respected?

Are they successful? If they are successful now, do you think that success will continue? If they are unsuccessful now, do you think they will *ever* enjoy success? Why or why not?

The humility around you: Now, as you think about someone around you who is humble, think about how they represent the four key characteristics of a humble person (being accountable; showing gratitude; smile; never rest on your success). Do they represent all four or just one or two? Are they permanently humble or do they just act with humility when it is convenient for them?

Most importantly, once they've started to represent humility (theoretically, after a lot of practice), do you think it is harder or easier for them to be humble?

Does humility become natural?

Expanding on humility: Certainly, on top of the four characteristics of humility covered in this session, there are plenty more.

Below, take a moment to brainstorm and expand upon one additional characteristic of humility. Maybe this is a characteristic that you already represent or maybe it's one that you would like to represent. What is it? And what can you do to practice embodying that characteristic?

In victory and defeat: Humility extends to situations when you win and when you lose. What will you do, moving forward, when you win and when you lose? Will you show gratitude? Will you appreciate those who have helped you get there and commit to working hard for future accomplishments?

Or will you rest on your success?

As you move forward, be mindful (ahead of time!) how you will react in both victory and defeat.

www.ingramcontent.com/pod-product-compliance
Lightning Source LLC
Chambersburg PA
CBHW080511110426
42742CB00017B/3068